BROADWAY MUSICAL TRIVIA BOOK

Fun-Filled Facts & Trivia Questions To Find Out How Much You Really Know!

By
KATIE SISON

D0972931

ISBN: 978-1-955149-01-3

Please consider writing a review!

Just visit: purplelink.org/review

TABLE OF CONTENTS

INTRODUCTION

Acknowledged today as one of the uniquely American art forms, musical theatre integrates multiple beloved forms of storytelling: song, dance, plot, character, and design. These individual artistic achievements come together to transport the audience to different worlds. We nervously step off our vessel with Anna Leonowens, clutching her son's hand in ours, ready to turn our lives upside down by going to live and teach in a foreign country. We snap and leap through the dangerous streets of New York City with the Jets and the Sharks, sticking with our gang but always on the lookout for a rumble. We trudge alongside Tevye and his family as we depart from the only home we've ever known, carrying whatever we can. Our dear friend Sophie reads to us from her mother's diary, revealing that there are three potential men who could be her father, and we squeal and flail our arms appropriately.

Though its roots can be traced back several millennia, musical theatre proper was born in New York City at the turn of the twentieth century. Its distinct sound developed out of partnerships between Black jazz artists and Jewish songwriters, and the art form would develop continuously throughout the twentieth century and into the twenty-first.

Musicals have long been a beloved part of American culture, and the beautiful songs and stories that have been introduced have touched millions around the world. Musical theatre has faced a resurgence in popularity in the last two decades, due in part to musicals with more contemporary music, like *Hamilton*, the popularity of TV shows that emphasize highly technical singing and dancing, like *American Idol*, *Glee*, and *Smash,* and the large number of musicals that have been adapted from movies or other popular source material, like *Mean Girls*, *Heathers*, and *Beetlejuice*. This trivia book, Broadway Trivia, highlights the interesting events, people, and shows that have impacted both the art form and us, the audience.

This trivia book begins with the precursors to musical theatre throughout the world and narrows to the island we will come back to time and time again: Manhattan. We explore each thrilling decade and then cover grander topics that span the years. Each chapter begins with a series of multiple-choice and true or false questions with the answers following on the next page. After testing your knowledge, peruse the "Did You Know" section for quirky anecdotes, fun facts, and important records to add to your knowledge.

Both the statistics and information reported in this book are recent and up-to-date as of March 2021. Broadway theaters closed on March 12, 2020, due to the COVID-19 pandemic, prematurely closing sixteen shows that were actively playing or beginning the process to open. The shutdown has been extended several times and is currently slated to end in June 2021. We all miss it terribly, and no one is sure what Broadway will look like when we come back, but theatre has adapted before and it will again.

In the meantime, test yourself on your knowledge of Broadway theatre! Whether you're a Fosse fan, more of a Golden-Age gal, or you cry yourself to sleep listening to *Next to Normal*, you'll strengthen your knowledge of the history of American musical theatre and the remarkable people who have made it happen.

Let's see how much you know about Broadway!

CHAPTER 1:

PRE-GOLDEN AGE

*"I regard theatre as the greatest of all art forms, the most
immediate way in which a human being can share with
another the sense of what it is to be a human being."*
- Oscar Wilde

TRIVIA TIME!

1. The earliest examples of music and dance being used in
    plays and large theatrical productions are often attributed
    to this country, which held yearly theatre festivals.

    a. Egypt
    b. Italy
    c. Greece ✓
    d. China

2. One recognizable antecedent of musical theatre featured
    clowns playing over-the-top, familiar stock characters like
    the conniving servant, the shrewish wife, or the gullible
    old man in this highly improvised art form that began in
    Rome.

a. Opera
b. Commedia dell'arte ✓
c. Improv comedy
d. Improviso dell'arte

3. Another precursor to musical theatre that began in Italy, this form of entertainment featured grand architectural sets and costume designs and was often performed for royalty, including England's Queen Elizabeth I.

a. Ballet
b. Allegory
c. Dumbshow
d. Masque ✓

4. True or False: The first documented long-running ✓ theatrical piece was Michael Balfe's *The Bohemian Girl.* F

5. Which century saw the birth of a significant theatre presence in America when a London businessman and his brother shipped a company of English actors across the pond?

a. 17th
b. 18th ✓
c. 19th
d. 20th

6. Inspired by French and Italian operetta, this famous English duo wrote a number of comic operas like *The Pirates of Penzance*, *The Mikado*, and *H.M.S. Pinafore.*

a. Harrigan and Hart
b. Offenbach and Strauss
c. Barnum and Keene
d. Gilbert and Sullivan ✓

7. In *The Pirates of Penzance*, Major-General Stanley sings that he is "the very model of a modern major-general" and that he possesses "information vegetable, animal, and mineral." Which two "historical" battles does he list as examples of his extensive military knowledge, which he describes as "categorical?"

    a. Marathon and Waterloo ✓
    b. Thermopylae and Hastings
    c. Agincourt and Tours
    d. Trafalgar and Troy

8. True or False: American vaudeville was advertised as the polite entertainment option. ✓

9. The father of American musical theatre sought to create a style distinct from the heavy influence of English comic operas. Who is this figure, the composer of songs like "You're a Grand Old Flag," "Over There," and "Give My Regards to Broadway"?

    a. John Philip Sousa
    b. Irving Berlin
    c. George M. Cohan ✓
    d. George Edwardes

10. At the time, this theatre was one of the smallest ones on Broadway, opening in 1913. A succession of sophisticated, witty musicals written by Jerome Kern, Guy Bolton, and P. G. Wodehouse were staged here during the early twentieth century.

    a. The Princess Theatre ✓
    b. The Queen's Theatre

c. The Schubert Theatre

d. The Comstock Theatre

11. Name this 1925 musical about a Bible publisher in the midst of a blackmail scheme and a newly-engaged Manhattan heiress who runs off to Atlantic City for a weekend of fun.

    a. *Lady, Be Good*

    b. *Irene*

    c. *Oh, Kay!*

    d. *No, No, Nanette* ✓

12. True or False: Fred Astaire's first dance partner was his sister Ann Astaire. ✓

13. Name the trio of brothers whose theatre-management company named after themselves owned 86 theaters by 1924, which caused the Actor's Equity union to be formed to balance their power?

    a. The Ziegfeld brothers

    b. The Shubert brothers ✓

    c. The Hays brothers

    d. The Winter brothers

14. What was the first Broadway musical with an all-Black cast and writing team, which opened in 1921 and was a smash hit, running for a record 484 performances?

    a. *Shuffle Along* ✓

    b. *Funny Face*

    c. *El Capitan*

    d. *A Trip to Chinatown*

15. *Babes in Arms, The Boys from Syracuse,* and *Pal Joey* are all written by this famous duo, who were known for the sense of adventure in their songs.

    a. The Gershwins
    b. Irving Berlin and Cole Porter
    c. Richard Rodgers and Oscar Hammerstein II
    d. Richard Rodgers and Lorenz Hart ✓

16. True or False: Tin Pan Alley, the central hub of the music publishing business in New York City around the turn of the twentieth century, was nicknamed in honor of a factory that had previously been located there. ✓

17. The musical *Anything Goes* by Cole Porter tells of leading man Billy Crocker and his efforts to win over Hope Harcourt, who is already engaged, with the help of *Public Enemy Number 13* gangster Moonface and this former evangelist became nightclub singer.

    a. Evelyn Oakleigh
    b. May Daly
    c. Reno Sweeney ✓
    d. Maria Ziegler

18. The undisputed First Lady of the musical comedy stage was originally known by her last name Zimmerman, which she changed to fit on a theater marquee. Who was this famous fiery-tempered singer and actress, known for originating the role of Annie Oakley in *Annie Get Your Gun*?

    a. Ruth Etting
    b. Ethel Merman ✓

c. Dixie Lee

d. Dorothy Zimmer

19. The premiere of this musical marked a change in the American musical theatre from lighthearted musical comedy to a combination of spectacle and serious subject matter. Which 1927 musical is set on the Mississippi River boat the Cotton Blossom?

   a. *Ol' Man River*
   b. *The James Adams Floating Palace Theatre*
   c. *Criss Cross*
   d. *Show Boat* ✓

20. True or False: The librettist of *Porgy and Bess*, which premiered in 1935 and featured a cast of classically trained Black singers, also wrote the 1925 novel of the same name.

ANSWERS

1. C - Greece

2. B - Commedia dell'arte

3. D - Masque

4. False! The first long-running theatrical piece was actually *The Beggar's Opera* by John Gay, which ran for 62 consecutive performances in 1728.

5. B - 18th

6. D - Gilbert and Sullivan

7. A - Marathon and Waterloo

8. True! This caused some theater managers to ban the use of words like "slob" while onstage and threaten to blacklist any performers caught using them.

9. C - George M. Cohan

10. A - The Princess Theatre

11. D - *No, No, Nanette*

12. False! His first dance partner was his sister, but her name was Adele and she went on to have her own career as a dancer.

13. B - The Shubert Brothers

14. A - *Shuffle Along*

15. D - Richard Rodgers and Lorenz Hart

16. False! There are several stories regarding the name, but the most popular is that it came from a rude comment in an article describing how the sound of multiple pianos playing different tunes at once sounded like the crashing of tin pans in an alley.

17. C - Reno Sweeney

18. B - Ethel Merman

19. D - *Show Boat*

20. True

DID YOU KNOW?

- Another early example of music and skit being used to tell a story was 12th and 13th-century liturgical dramas, which would often include chanting and poetic recitations done by a troupe of actors out of a large wagon.

- The first musical to surpass 500 performances was *The Chimes of Normandy*, a French operetta, in 1878.

- Times Square may be the center of Broadway now, but theatre in New York City was performed largely downtown until the second half of the nineteenth century when it began to shift slowly north toward midtown; it would not arrive in the Times Square area until the 1920s and 30s.

- Shows performed in the United States tended to run for shorter lengths of time than shows performed in England, but in 1891, *A Trip to Chinatown* ran for 657 performances. It held that record until 1919, when *Irene* surpassed it with 670 performances.

- Theatre attendance was driven up by the United States entering into World War I in 1917. Musical comedy offered escapism to the public, with song-and-dance revues like the *Ziegfeld Follies* that featured elaborate costumes, beautiful chorus girls, and entertainers like Josephine Baker, W. C. Fields, and Fanny Brice.

- The popularity of British musical theatre in the United States waned after World War I and was gradually replaced by musical theatre that integrated ragtime and jazz, musical styles which more accurately represented the bustling twentieth century than the grand operatic styles of Europe.

- "Someone to Watch Over Me" by George and Ira Gershwin is one of the most famous twentieth-century torch songs, covered by artists like Frank Sinatra, Barbra Streisand, Elton John, and Amy Winehouse, but it was originally written by George Gershwin as a quick, up-tempo swing tune.

- In 1931, another Gershwin musical, the political satire *Of Thee I Sing*, became the first musical to be awarded the Pulitzer Prize. The musical is about the presidential race of candidate John P. Wintergreen, who holds a pageant to determine the most beautiful girl in the country to be his wife since he is running on the platform of love.

- *The Threepenny Opera*, adapted from John Gay's *The Beggar Opera* by German playwright Bertolt Brecht and German composer Kurt Weill, offers a Socialist critique of the capitalist world. Its name comes from Brecht's premise that the opera should be "as splendid as only beggars can imagine and yet cheap enough for beggars to be able to watch." Despite its great success in Germany in 1928, it was not introduced to the United States until the film version was released in 1931, and the 1933 Broadway production closed after twelve performances.

- The first time a Black actor appeared in a show with white actors was in 1933, when Ethel Waters starred in *As Thousands Cheer*, a revue by Irving Berlin and Moss Hart where each song and skit was based on a different newspaper headline.

- The first resident professional theatre founded in the United States was The Cleveland Playhouse, which opened in 1921.

CHAPTER 2:

THE 1940S

"The theatre is so endlessly fascinating because it's so accidental. It's so much like life." - Arthur Miller

TRIVIA TIME!

1. A musical that fully integrates song, character, plot, and dance to further the plot and heighten the emotion of the story rather than just play for laughs or applause is referred to as what kind of musical?

    a. Straight musical
    b. Book musical √
    c. Modern musical
    d. Golden Age musical

2. The Tony Awards are named for this co-founder of the American Theatre Wing.

    a. Antoinette Perry ⌡
    b. Anthony Pemberton
    c. Jacob Tony
    d. Anthony Burton

3. Which 1943 musical sees the curtain rise at the beginning of Act One on Aunt Eller churning butter while an acappella baritone voice sings from offstage, rather than a group of high-kicking chorus girls, the standard of the time?

    a. *The Merry Widow*
    b. *Carmen Jones*
    c. *Oklahoma!* ✓
    d. *One Touch of Venus*

4. Her father and uncle were both Hollywood directors, and her first choreography gig on the movie *Cleopatra* ended with her leaving the film due to creative differences. Who is this Golden Age choreographer, known for her strong character work grounded in classic ballet?

    a. Agnes DeMille ✓
    b. Albertina Rasch
    c. Catherine Littlefield
    d. Helen Tamiris

5. True or False: Lyricist and librettist Oscar Hammerstein II won all three Academy Awards he was nominated for during the 1940s.

6. Which jaunty, toe-tapping musical about three American sailors on shore leave with a score by Leonard Bernstein was the first musical collaboration between Betty Comden and Adolph Green?

    a. *Up in Central Park*
    b. *Follow the Girls*
    c. *Fancy Free*
    d. *On the Town*

7. Richard Rodgers' favorite of his musicals, *Carousel*, tells the tragic story of carnival barker Billy Bigelow and mill worker Julie Jordan. A secondary plot line follows Carrie Pipperidge and her romance with "an almost perfect beau" who always smells like fish. Who is Carrie's "young sea-faring, bold and daring, big bewhiskered, overbearing darling?"

   a. Mister Snow ✓
   b. Mister Green
   c. Mister Dailey
   d. Mister May

8. *Annie Get Your Gun*, which tells the story of famous marksman Annie Oakley, was one of two musicals written by Irving Berlin for Ethel Merman. The project originally had another composer slated, but he, unfortunately, passed away on November 5, 1945, due to a brain hemorrhage. Who was this composer, whose work includes musicals like *Roberta* and *Show Boat* and the film *Swing Time*?

   a. Otto Harbach
   b. Seymour Hicks
   c. Jerome Kern ✓
   d. Ivan Caryll

9. True or False: The original 1947 production of *Finian's Rainbow*, a musical about two Irish immigrants in the hilariously named state of Missitucky, featured a supporting actor wearing blackface. ✗

10. The musical *Brigadoon* features two American tourists who stumble upon a mysterious village in the Scottish Highlands that only appears one day every one-hundred

years. Which two frequent collaborators provided the music, lyrics, and book?

   a. Richard Rodgers and Oscar Hammerstein II
   b. Alan Jay Lerner and Frederick Loewe √
   c. Richard Rodgers and Lorenz Hart
   d. Alan Jay Lerner and Kurt Weill

11. True or False: Famous ballet choreographer George Balanchine provided the choreography for several Broadway musicals as well. ✕

12. Which Rodgers and Hammerstein musical was directed by Agnes DeMille?

   a. *Carousel*
   b. *South Pacific*
   c. *The King and I*
   d. *Allegro* √

13. The ladies mentioned in this song from Cole Porter's *Kiss Me, Kate* include Momo from Milano, Lucretia from Pompeii, Rebecca from Ponte Vecchio, and Fedora, who has "a gangster sister from Chicago." Name this funny tune, sung in Act Two by Fred Graham.

   a. "Where Is The Life That Late I Led?" √
   b. "Why Can't You Behave?"
   c. "Too Darn Hot"
   d. "Always True to You in My Fashion"

14. Which William Shakespeare comedy was adapted into *Kiss Me Kate*, where Petruchio is convinced by his friend Hortensio to woo Bianca's older sister Katarina, who is

rude and assertive but must marry before her younger sister may?

    a. *Much Ado About Nothing*
    b. *Two Gentlemen of Verona*
    c. *The Taming of the Shrew* ✓
    d. *A Comedy of Errors*

15. Part of the success of Golden Age musicals can be attributed to their alignment with the public's perceptions of The American Dream. Which one of these beliefs was not reflected in the Broadway musicals of the time?

    a. The self-made American spirit
    b. Stability defined by loving relationships ending in marriage
    c. The function of women as homemaker and mother
    d. None of the above ✓

16. In *South Pacific*, Rodgers and Hammerstein explore the dangers of racial prejudice in two relationships between Lieutenant Joseph Cable and Liat, a young Tonkinese woman, and wealthy plantation owner Emile de Becque and this U.S. Navy nurse, who refuses to marry Emile when she learns he has two biracial children from his first marriage.

    a. Kitty Verdun
    b. Nellie Forbush ✓
    c. Evelina Applegate
    d. Della Green

17. Which operatic Italian bass originated the role of Emile de Becque after retiring from New York's Metropolitan Opera with 95 roles to his name?

a. Giovanni Martinelli

b. Lawrence Tibbett

c. Giuseppe De Luca

d. Ezio Pinza √

18. True or False: Carol Channing's first Broadway role was in the 1948 satirical musical revue *Lend an Ear*.

19. He got his start dancing in Broadway-style revues in the Poconos, but it was his work for *On the Town* that launched his career as one of the most influential Broadway choreographers of all time. Who is this man, who famously once toppled backward into the orchestra pit while giving directions to his dancers?

a. Bobby Connolly

b. Jack Cole

c. Jerome Robbins √

d. Robert Alton

20. The movie version starred Marilyn Monroe, but the role of Lorelei Lee was originated onstage by a different actress who later performed the same role in a different Broadway adaptation of the 1925 novel. Name this 1949 Broadway production that introduced the song "Diamonds Are a Girl's Best Friend."

a. *One Touch of Venus*

b. *Gentlemen Prefer Blondes* √

c. *Bloomer Girl*

d. *Call Me Madam*

21. True or False: Jule Styne spent most of the 1940s as a vocal coach to the stars for 20th Century Fox.

ANSWERS

1. B - Book musical

2. A - Antoinette Perry

3. C - *Oklahoma!*

4. A - Agnes DeMille

5. False! Though he was nominated for three, he only won two.

6. D - *On the Town*

7. A - Mister Snow

8. C - Jerome Kern

9. True! Contemporary productions of *Finian's Rainbow* typically used two actors for the role of Senator Rawkins.

10. B - Alan Jay Lerner and Frederick Loewe

11. True! His choreography would go on to inspire Jerome Robbins, who danced in

12. Balanchine's chorus in two different productions.

13. D - *Allegro*

14. A - "Where Is The Life That Late I Led?"

15. C - *The Taming of the Shrew*

16. D - None of the above

17. B - Nellie Forbush

18. D - Ezio Pinza

19. False! She was the understudy for Eve Arden in *Let's Face It!* in 1941.

20. C - Jerome Robbins

21. B - *Gentlemen Prefer Blondes*

22. False! 20th Century Fox cut back on their vocal coaches in 1941, and Styne focused on writing songs for films.

DID YOU KNOW?

- *Kiss Me, Kate* was the first production to win the Tony Award for Best Musical at its inaugural ceremony in 1947.

- *South Pacific* remains the only musical production to win all four acting categories at the Tony Awards (Best Performance by a Leading Actor in a Musical, Best Performance by a Leading Actress in a Musical, Best Performance by a Featured Actor in a Musical, and Best Performance by a Featured Actress in a Musical).

- Cole Porter's 1940 musical *Panama Hattie*, in which a nightclub owner with a heart of gold must win the approval of her fiancé's eight-year-old daughter, was the first show for which Ethel Merman received solo star billing; it was also the longest-running of the five Porter shows that featured her.

- The only Broadway musical that film star Gene Kelly played a major role in was *Pal Joey*, which was based on a series of *New Yorker* short stories with music from Rodgers and Hart. However, the film version produced in 1957 featured Frank Sinatra instead.

- The 1942 musical *By Jupiter* was at the time the longest-running Rodgers and Hart musical; it would also be their last new collaboration together due to Hart's death in 1943.

- Irving Berlin put together the all-soldier revue *This Is the Army* as a benefit for the Army Emergency Relief Fund during World War II. It was filmed in 1943, featuring an ensemble cast including future president of the United States, Ronald Reagan.

- The lyrics for Kurt Weill's music for *One Touch of Venus* were provided by American poet Ogden Nash who is best known for his humorous couplets.

- In 1943, Oscar Hammerstein II took Georges Bizet's opera *Carmen* and set it in the World War II-era; the cigarette factory became a parachute factory, the bullfighter Escamillo became the boxer Husky Miller, and the musical used an all-Black cast. A film version was made in 1954 starring Dorothy Dandridge.

- Due to the rise in popularity of book musicals and television, traditional revues began to lose their large, receptive audiences toward the end of the decade. *Make Mine Manhattan* played for 429 performances in 1948 and marked the end of the pre-Golden Age era of lighthearted satire vignettes loosely connected by theme and song.

- Kurt Weill's extensive Broadway career came to an end in 1949 with the production of *Lost in the Stars*, a musical adaptation of Alan Paton's *Cry, the Beloved Country* which tells the story of Absalom Kumalo, the son of a Black minister who accidentally kills a white man during an attempted robbery in apartheid South Africa.

CHAPTER 3:

THE 1950S

"The theatre is a spiritual and social x-ray of its time.
The theatre was created to tell people the truth about life
and the social situation." - Stella Adler

TRIVIA TIME!

1. True or False: *Guys and Dolls* won the Pulitzer Prize for Drama in 1951.

2. The 1955 film adaptation of *Guys and Dolls* starred Marlon Brando, Jean Simmons, Vivian Blaine, and Frank Sinatra. Which "good old reliable" gambler did Sinatra play, who tries to organize an illegal craps game under the nose of the police all while his fiancée of fourteen years wants him to marry her and go straight?

   a. Sky Masterson
   b. Nicely-Nicely Johnson
   c. Harry the Horse
   d. Nathan Detroit

3. When told he would need to shave his head for the role of the King of Siam in the Broadway production of *The King and I*, this actor initially refused, convinced he would look terrible. The look later became his trademark. Who is this Russian-American actor who reprised his role as the King of Siam in the 1956 film, becoming one of the only actors to win both a Tony Award and an Academy Award for the same role?

   a. Rex Harrison
   b. Yul Brynner
   c. Michael Chekhov
   d. Mikhail Baryshnikov

4. Lerner and Loewe's *My Fair Lady* was adapted from a George Bernard Shaw play, which took its title from the Greek myth of a sculptor who fell in love with one of his statues, which then came to life. Who was this sculptor who fell in love with the statue Galatea?

   a. Daedalus
   b. Talos
   c. Pygmalion
   d. Hephaestus

5. Which English actress of both stage and screen fame made her Broadway debut in the 1954 musical *The Boy Friend*?

   a. Julie Andrews
   b. Gertrude Lawrence
   c. Angela Lansbury
   d. Vivien Leigh

6. Which 1959 musical featured music from Jule Styne, lyrics from Stephen Sondheim, and was called "Broadway's own brassy, unlikely answer to King Lear" by critic Frank Rich?

   a. *Fiorello!*
   b. *The Sound of Music*
   c. *Gypsy* ✓
   d. *Redhead*

7. Carol Burnett originated the role of Princess Winnifred the Woebegone in *Once Upon a Mattress*, a retelling of Hans Christian Andersen's "The Princess and the Pea." In the musical, we are introduced to the unrefined and rowdy Winnifred when she swims the castle moat. What ironic adjective does she use to describe herself to the kingdom?

   a. "Quiet"
   b. "Dainty"
   c. "Meek"
   d. "Shy" ✓

8. The music for this song is provided by Leonard Bernstein and the lyrics by Stephen Sondheim. Which comedic number from *West Side Story* was censored by Columbia Records, leading to a different final lyric which Sondheim insists is the best in the musical?

   a. "Gee, Officer Krupke" ✓
   b. "Cool"
   c. "I Feel Pretty"
   d. "Jet Song"

9. Puerto Rican actress Rita Moreno won an Academy Award for her portrayal of Anita in the film version of

West Side Story, but the role was originated on Broadway by a different Puerto Rican actress. Name this actress, whose first theatrical role was in the touring company of *Call Me Madam*.

    a. Carol Lawrence
    b. Marlys Watters
    c. Luba Lisa
    d. Chita Rivera

10. True or False: *The Music Man* took eight years for Meredith Willson to write.

11. For which of her lyrical Broadway roles did Barbara Cook win a Tony Award?

    a. Cunegonde
    b. Sandy
    c. Marian Paroo
    d. Hilda Miller

12. *Candide*, an operetta composed by Leonard Bernstein and based on the Voltaire novella of the same name, is generally performed with a book by Hugh Wheeler, but the libretto was originally provided by another writer. Which playwright's book was featured in the original 1956 production?

    a. Rachel Wilbur
    b. Dorothy Parker
    c. Myra Page
    d. Lillian Hellman

13. Eartha Kitt may be best known today for singing "Santa Baby" in the filmed version of the revue *New Faces of 1952*

that she starred in on Broadway, but her first Broadway role was actually as "the face that launched a thousand ships," Helen of Troy, in a staging of *Dr. Faustus* by which famous actor and filmmaker?

a. Don Siegel
b. Orson Welles ✓
c. Woody Allen
d. Elia Kazan

14. What 1953 musical is generally considered the successor to *On the Town*, as the score was written by the same team of Leonard Bernstein, Betty Comden, and Adolph Green and the show once again portrayed New York City as just about the happiest, friendliest place on earth?

a. *Two on the Aisle*
b. *Bells Are Ringing*
c. *Wonderful Town* ✓
d. *Do Re Mi*

15. True or False: Betty Comden and Adolph Green's writing partnership lasted sixty years. ✗

16. Which Rodgers and Hammerstein musical that premiered in 1958 (but is rarely performed today) was directed by Gene Kelly in his stage directorial debut?

a. *Flower Drum Song* ✓
b. *State Fair*
c. *Me and Juliet*
d. *Pipe Dream*

17. *Damn Yankees*, which premiered in 1955 at the 46th Street Theatre, is a modern retelling of what fiendish legend?

a. Sir Gawain and the Green Knight
b. Daedalus and Icarus
c. Dracula
d. Faust ✓

18. Bob Fosse insisted on meeting and working with the actress who the producers hoped to cast as Lola in the original Broadway production of *Damn Yankees,* who he would go on to marry in 1960. Who is this red-haired triple threat, who won a Tony Award for her performance?

a. Gwen Verdon ✓
b. Mitzi Gaynor
c. Shirley MacLaine
d. Ann Reinking

19. Though her career in the theatre spanned fifty years, two of the roles that defined her as an actress premiered in the 1950s. Who is this Tony Award-winning actress, best known for originating the roles of Maria von Trapp and Peter Pan?

a. Julie Andrews
b. Mary Martin ✓
c. Gertrude Lawrence
d. Patricia Wilson

20. True or False: Jerome Robbins is known as the Father of Theatrical Jazz Dance.

ANSWERS

1. False! *Guys and Dolls* was actually selected to be the winner, but the selection was vetoed due to the suspected Communist sympathies of book writer Abe Burrows. No Pulitzer Prize for Drama was awarded that year.

2. D - Nathan Detroit

3. B - Yul Brynner

4. C - Pygmalion

5. A - Julie Andrews

6. C - *Gypsy*

7. D - "Shy"

8. A - "Gee, Officer Krupke"

9. D - Chita Rivera

10. True! Meredith Willson began to develop the musical in his 1948 memoir *And There I Stood With My Piccolo*.

11. C - Marian Paroo

12. D - Lillian Hellman

13. B - Orson Welles

14. C - *Wonderful Town*

15. True! It is sometimes referred to as "the longest-running creative partnership in theatre history."

16. A - *Flower Drum Song*

17. D - Faust

18. A - Gwen Verdon

19. B - Mary Martin

20. False! That title belongs to dancer and choreographer Jack Cole.

DID YOU KNOW?

- *Guys and Dolls* was the fifth longest-running Broadway musical of the 1950s.

- Despite its heartwarming and clever score by Harold Rome, its cast of established and hard-working actors, and a director who would not stop striving to improve the show even after opening night, the Broadway musical *Wish You Were Here* is mostly known now as "the musical with the swimming pool."

- Betty Comden and Adolph Green were brought into the writing process of *Wonderful Town* only about five weeks before rehearsals since they were taking over from the previous lyricists who quit the project due to a conflict with the librettists.

- On opening night of Cole Porter's *Can-Can* the musical, Gwen Verdon, who sang only a little but danced the remarkable "Garden of Eden" ballet, was brought from her dressing room in a towel to take a curtain call.

- British writers of musicals went without much success for a long time in New York; though composer and lyricist Sandy Wilson managed to achieve acclaim, to date only one of his musicals, *The Boy Friend*, has been produced on Broadway, which premiered in 1954.

- *House of Flowers*, a 1954 Broadway production with a score by Harold Arlen and a book by Truman Capote, was inspired by Capote's 1948 voyage to Port-au-Prince, Haiti and his visits to the local bordellos.

- The 1955 production of *Plain and Fancy* used a similar plot device to *Brigadoon*, but instead of traveling to Scotland, the two cosmopolitan New Yorkers in this musical travel instead to Pennsylvania to meet with a community of Amish farmers.

- Cole Porter's last Broadway musical was *Silk Stockings*, which enjoyed a short Broadway run before being adapted into a 1957 film starring Fred Astaire and Cyd Charisse.

- The 1956 musical *Bells Are Ringing* about a chatty telephone operator played by Judy Holliday had the longest run of the eight musicals from the writing team of Jule Styne, Betty Comden, and Adolph Green.

- While Leonard Bernstein received much acclaim for his score, the initial production of *Candide* lasted less than three months, at seventy-three performances.

- *West Side Story* is about the blossoming romance between Maria, a Puerto Rican girl, and Tony, a white boy, but the original project was titled *East Side Story* and set up the conflict between a Jewish boy and an Italian Catholic girl who fall in love and want to get married. Scheduling conflicts caused the project to be tabled for six years, and the premise seemed dated when the writing team returned to it.

CHAPTER 4:

THE 1960S

"Hey, mama, welcome to the 60's!" - Hairspray

TRIVIA TIME!

1. *Bye Bye Birdie*, produced in 1960, was the earliest musical about the phenomenon of rock-and-roll and its effect on the American youth. What famous American actor and comedian was given the lead of Albert Peterson after auditioning for a smaller role?

    a. Peter Marshall
    b. Gene Rayburn
    c. Michael J. Pollard
    d. Dick van Dyke ✓

2. Whose career was launched by directing and choreographing *Bye Bye Birdie*, the first of nine book musicals he would direct during his career?

    a. Joe Layton
    b. Gower Champion ✓
    c. Jerome Robbins
    d. Bob Fosse

3. What late-nineteenth-century play by French playwright Edmond Rostand was the inspiration for the musical *The Fantasticks*?

    a. *Cyrano de Bergerac*
    b. *Les Romanesques* ✓
    c. *L'Aiglon*
    d. *Chantecler*

4. The title role was originated by Tammy Grimes on Broadway and played by Debbie Reynolds in the movie. Fresh off his success from *The Music Man*, Meredith Willson wrote a rousing score for which musical about an American socialite and philanthropist?

    a. *The Unsinkable Molly Brown* ✓
    b. *Irma La Douce*
    c. *Hello, Dolly!*
    d. *Sweet Charity*

5. Which 1960 musical from the writing team of Lerner and Loewe had the biggest advance sale of tickets in Broadway history at that time?

    a. *My Fair Lady*
    b. *Gigi*
    c. *Camelot* ✓
    d. *Life of the Party*

6. The role of King Arthur in *Camelot* was originated by this Welsh actor, famous for his Shakespearean roles and once called "the natural successor to [actor Laurence] Olivier."

    a. Robert Goulet
    b. Richard Greene

    c. Peter O'Toole

    d. Richard Burton ✓

7. True or False: The plot of *How to Succeed in Business Without Really Trying* is based on the satirical instruction manual of the same name by Shepherd Mead. F

8. Zero Mostel, Nathan Lane, and Whoopi Goldberg have all played the main character of this 1962 musical with a title derived from the first line of a story told by vaudeville comedians.

    a. *Stop the World - I Want to Get Off*

    b. *The Roar of the Greasepaint - The Smell of the Crowd*

    c. *Do I Hear a Waltz?*

    d. *A Funny Thing Happened on the Way to the Forum* ✓

9. Seven of this man's Tony Awards were awarded during the 1960s, for productions of *Fiorello!*, *A Funny Thing Happened on the Way to the Forum*, *Fiddler on the Roof*, and *Cabaret*. Name this giant of the American musical theatre!

    a. Stephen Sondheim

    b. Hal Prince ✓

    c. Bob Fosse

    d. Jack Cole

10. The 1963 Broadway transfer of *Oliver!* saw Lionel Bart win a Tony Award for Best Original Score, including songs like "I'd Do Anything," "As Long As He Needs Me," and this jaunty number, where the artful dodger welcomes poor orphan Oliver into the fold and offers him his friendship.

    a. "You've Got to Pick A Pocket Or Two"

    b. "Be Back Soon"

(c.) "Consider Yourself"
d. "It's a Fine Life"

11. Which musical saw Barbara Cook and Daniel Massey star as two bickering coworkers who are secretly romantic pen pals through a lonely-hearts ad? The 1963 Broadway production was directed by Hal Prince with a score by Sheldon Harnick and Jerry Bock.

    a. *She Loves Me* ✓
    b. *Tenderloin*
    c. *The Apple Tree*
    d. *Man in the Moon*

12. Though Lucille Ball played the role in the 1974 film, the 1966 Broadway production featured this actress in the role of the middle-aged, matchmaking widow Mame Dennis, which won her a Tony Award for Best Performance by a Leading Actress in a Musical.

    a. Bea Arthur
    b. Carol Channing
    c. Julie Andrews
    d. Angela Lansbury ∫

13. In the 1969 Broadway musical *1776*, we are introduced to the character of John Adams during the Second Continental Congress as he begs for the other delegates to vote yes for independence, only for them to complain about the heat and tell him, again and again, to do what?

    a. "Be quiet, Adams."
    b. "Take your seat."
    c. "Sit down, John." ✓
    d. "Clear the floor, please."

14. The plot of the 1964 musical *Fiddler on the Roof* was based on Sholem Aleichem's short stories about Tevye the Dairyman but the title of the play is inspired by another Russian-born Jewish artist. Who painted *The Fiddler*, *Green Violinist*, and *Le Mort*, which all feature a fiddler on a roof?

    a. Marc Chagall ✓
    b. Chaïm Soutine
    c. Sonia Delaunay
    d. El Lissitzsky

15. True or False: The first person to give the nickname *Zero* to actor Samuel Mostel was his mother Celia. ✓

16. Which musical was the first example of the rock musical and the first fully realized concept musical, which was produced on Broadway in 1968 and has been called "one of the last Broadway musicals to saturate the culture as shows from the golden age regularly did?"

    a. *High Spirits*
    b. *Hair* ✓
    c. *Cabaret*
    d. *Golden Boy*

17. The role of Fanny Brice in *Funny Girl* was refused by several established actresses like Mary Martin, Carol Channing, and Anne Bancroft. The role was eventually given to which famous American songstress?

    a. Bette Midler
    b. Liza Minnelli
    c. Judy Garland
    d. Barbra Streisand ✓

18. *110 in the Shade* takes place during a drought in the American southwest and centers the relationship between the spinster Lizzie Curry and a smooth-talking con-man named Bill Starbuck. N. Richard Nash, who wrote the original play, also wrote the book for the musical, which has a score by which writing team that also wrote *The Fantasticks*?

   a. Harvey Schmidt and Tom Jones ✓
   b. Jule Styne and Stephen Sondheim
   c. John Kander and Fred Ebb
   d. Sheldon Harnick and Jerry Bock

19. The 1960 revue *From A to Z* was considered a critical and commercial failure but it did premiere the work of a few rising stars who would go onto great success: actress Virginia Westoff, writer Woody Allen, composer Fred Ebb, and this composer, who wrote the scores for *Mame* and *Hello, Dolly!*

   a. Clark Gesner
   b. Cy Coleman
   c. Jerry Herman ✓
   d. Mitch Leigh

20. True or False: The original lyricist of *Man of La Mancha* was Joe Darion.

21. Kander and Ebb's portrait of Weimar era Germany *Cabaret* features a love story between the landlady Fraülein Schneider and Herr Schultz, an elderly Jewish man who owns a fruit shop. In their duet "It Couldn't Please Me More," what fruit does Herr Schultz given to Fraülein Schneider that gives the song its other name?

a. Banana
b. Pineapple ✓
c. Pear
d. Grapes

ANSWERS

1. D - Dick van Dyke

2. B - Gower Champion

3. B - *Les Romanesques*

4. A - *The Unsinkable Molly Brown*

5. C - *Camelot*

6. D - Richard Burton

7. False! The plot actually comes from an unproduced play by Jack Weinstock and Willie Gilbert.

8. D - *A Funny Thing Happened on the Way to the Forum*

9. B - Hal Prince

10. C - "Consider Yourself"

11. A - *She Loves Me*

12. D - Angela Lansbury

13. C - "Sit down, John."

14. A - Marc Chagall

15. True! According to Mostel's brother Bill, it was meant to chastise him into doing better at school.

16. B - *Hair*

17. D - Barbra Streisand

18. A - Harvey Schmidt and Tom Jones

19. Jerry Herman

20. False! The original lyricist was actually British poet W. H. Auden, whose lyrics were replaced by Darion's due to their satirical nature which criticized the audience.

21. B - Pineapple

DID YOU KNOW?

- *Hello, Dolly!* was nominated for eleven Tony Awards in 1964; it won ten of them (all except Best Performance by a Featured Actor in a Musical) which set a record that would hold for 37 years.

- After Jerome Robbins left the project due to differences with the book writer, *Funny Girl's* next director was Garson Kanin. Several of his decisions were very unpopular with the cast, especially Barbra Streisand, who demanded that Robbins return to the project after Kanin suggested that the song "People" be cut from the show.

- The song "Consider Yourself" from *Oliver!* was translated into Japanese and played to welcome Emperor Hirohito to Central Park in New York City when he came to visit the United States in 1975 at the invitation of President Gerald Ford.

- In 1960, the musical *Fiorello!* which chronicled the early career of New York City Mayor LaGuardia became the third musical to win the Pulitzer Prize for Drama.

- *She Loves Me* enjoyed a modest run when it was first produced on Broadway, but its 2016 revival made history as the first time a Broadway show was ever broadcast live.

- Scene Three of *1776*, between "The Lees of Old Virginia" and "But Mr. Adams," holds the record for the longest period in a musical without any singing or music, over thirty minutes. The musicians in the orchestra were permitted to leave the orchestra pit during the scene each night. This led to some criticism that the show was more of a play with music than a musical.

- The original 1964 Broadway production of *Fiddler on the Roof* made history as the first musical to perform for over 3,000 performances. It held that record for nearly ten years until it was surpassed by *Grease*.

- The world's longest-running musical to this day is *The Fantasticks*. The original off-Broadway production ran for 42 years and did not close until 2002.

- The musical *Camelot*, which was based on T. H. White's novel *The Once and Future King*, was originally titled *Jenny Kissed Me*.

- In 1962, *How to Succeed in Business Without Really Trying* was awarded the Pulitzer Prize for Drama, making it the fourth musical to be awarded the honor.

- "Comedy Tonight" is the well-known witty opening number of *A Funny Thing Happened on the Way to the Forum*, but the original opening number was titled "Love is in the Air." That number was cut from the show when Jerome Robbins was brought in to fix the show, which was not doing well in out-of-town tryouts.

CHAPTER 5:

THE 1970S

"There's theater in life, obviously, and there's life in theater." - Charlie Kaufman

TRIVIA TIME!

1. Which American actor originated the role of high-school greaser Danny Zuko in the 1972 stage production of *Grease*, which earned him a Tony Award nomination for Best Performance by a Leading Actor in a Musical?

    a. John Travolta
    b. Barry Bostwick ✓
    c. Doug Stevenson
    d. Richard Gere

2. In the musical *Chicago*, Amos Hart supports his wife Roxie after she murders her ex-lover Fred, even when he finds out that she may be pregnant with Fred's child. What song does Amos sing in Act Two bemoaning how no matter what he does for others, they never seem to notice him?

    a. "All I Care About"
    b. "Funny Honey"

c. "I Can't Do It Alone"

d. "Mr. Cellophane"

3. True or False: *A Chorus Line* originally had a different ending, where the dancers who were chosen for the ensemble would change each night depending on the actor's individual performance during that run.

4. Which American singer, songwriter, and actress originated the role of Dorothy in the 1975 Broadway production of *The Wiz*, a retelling of L. Frank Baum's novel *The Wonderful Wizard of Oz* that focused on contemporary African-American culture?

   a. Stephanie Mills

   b. Renee C. Harris

   c. Deborah Malone

   d. Tasha Scott

5. In the musical *Pippin*, the title character seeks out the meaning of life by trying all sorts of things, including a life with the Church, education at the University of Padua, and a free-for-all with the pleasures of life recommended to him by his grandmother Berthe. Which famous television actress originated the role of Berthe in the 1972 production?

   a. Dorothy Stickney

   b. Irene Ryan

   c. Bea Benaderet

   d. Patricia Elliott

6. True or False: The musical *Godspell* was created as a series of skits performed by student religious life at Carnegie-Mellon University.

7. The musical *Godspell* was based on which New Testament Gospel from the Bible?

    a. Gospel of Matthew
    b. Gospel of Mark
    c. Gospel of Luke
    d. Gospel of John

8. Which actress originated the role of the little orphan herself in the 1977 musical *Annie* that was based on Harold Gray's comic strip?

    a. Sarah Jessica Parker
    b. Kristen Vigard
    c. Allison Smith
    d. Andrea McArdle

9. The 1978 revue *Ain't Misbehavin'* was a tribute to the Black jazz artists and musicians who took part in the Harlem Renaissance in the 1920s and 1930s, and its title came from a song by which famous jazz pianist and composer?

    a. Earl Hines
    b. Fats Waller
    c. Count Basie
    d. James P. Johnson

10. His Broadway debut was in the 1973 science fiction play *Warp!,* and he originated the title character of *The Wiz* in 1975. He received a Drama Desk Award nomination for his performance in *Ain't Misbehavin'*, which ran for over 1,600 performances. Name this actor!

    a. Ken Page
    b. Ted Ross

c. André DeShields

d. Hinton Battle

11. Though he was nominated at the Tony Awards for his performance as Judas Iscariot in *Jesus Christ Superstar* in 1972, this actor won his Tony Award the next year in 1973 for his role as the Leading Player in *Pippin*. Who is this American triple threat?

a. Ben Vereen

b. Murray Head

c. Larry Riley

d. Stephen Tate

12. True or False: Andrew Lloyd Webber and Tim Rice intended for the Greek chorus character of Che in *Evita* to be based upon controversial Marxist Argentine revolutionary Che Guevara.

13. Which Broadway actress earned acclaim for her turn as Val in *A Chorus Line* singing "Dance: 10; Looks: 3" and a Drama Desk Award nomination for her performance as Amber in the 1978 production of *The Best Little Whorehouse in Texas*?

a. Linda Williams

b. Ann Reinking

c. Mitzi Hamilton

d. Pamela Blair

14. In 1974, at the age of only twenty-six, composer Stephen Schwartz had three successful musicals playing in New York City simultaneously: *Godspell*, *Pippin*, and this lesser-known musical, which takes place in a seedy nightclub called The Top Hat.

a. *The Survival of St. Joan*

b. *The Magic Show*

c. *The Baker's Wife*

d. *Working*

15. True or False: "Herod's Song" from *Jesus Christ Superstar* was a rewrite of a song that Andrew Lloyd Webber and Tim Rice had written a few years before to enter into the Eurovision Song Contest.

16. Stephen Sondheim's musical *Follies* tells the story of a reunion of the former performers of a musical revue based on the *Ziegfeld Follies*. What is the name of the theater that is soon to be demolished where the action takes place?

a. The Schubert Theatre

b. The Heinman Theatre

c. The Weismann Theatre

d. The Winter Garden Theatre

17. In 1971, the Tony Award for Best Original Score was split into two categories: Best Score and Best Lyrics. Which musical written by Stephen Sondheim won him both Best Score and Best Lyrics that year?

a. *Follies*

b. *A Little Night Music*

c. *Sweeney Todd: The Demon Barber of Fleet Street*

d. *Company*

18. What European country provides the setting for Stephen Sondheim's *A Little Night Music*?

a. Italy

b. Sweden

c. Finland

d. Germany

19. One of Stephen Sondheim's least-performed musicals chronicles 127 years of Westernization in Japan. Its title comes from a phrase used in an 1853 letter from Admiral Matthew Perry addressed to the Japanese Emperor. Which 1976 musical was staged kabuki-style and closed after six months, despite being nominated for ten Tony Awards?

a. *The Undersigned*

b. *The Ensuing Spring*

c. *Your Imperial Majesty*

d. *Pacific Overtures*

20. The title character of *Sweeney Todd* is able to accomplish many of his goals thanks to the assistance from his former landlady, the cheerful yet amoral Mrs. Lovett, who is in love with Sweeney and dreams of moving away from London to live in the country in what song from Act Two?

a. "By the Sea"

b. "Ooh, Mr. Todd!"

c. "Just You and Me and the English Channel"

d. "In a House of Our Own"

21. Though she never won a Tony Award for Best Choreography, she was nominated four times during the 1970s, including for *Grease* and *Pacific Overtures*. Who is this choreographer, whose Broadway debut was as the tomboy Anybodys in *West Side Story*?

a. Maxine Gordon

b. Patricia Birch

c. Graciela Daniele

d. Edie Cowan

22. Though Len Cariou is best known in American musical theatre for playing the roles of Fredrik and Sweeney Todd, his first Tony nomination was for a role he played opposite Lauren Bacall in *Applause,* the musical adaptation of what film?

    a. *The Barefoot Contessa*
    b. *The Bad and the Beautiful*
    c. *Rear Window*
    d. *All About Eve*

23. Which actress did Stephen Sondheim write his most famous song "Send in the Clowns" for, who originated the role of Desiree Armfeldt in *A Little Night Music*?

    a. Glynis Johns
    b. Judy Collins
    c. Jean Simmons
    d. Judi Dench

24. In 1975, twenty-four year old Patti LuPone earned her first Tony Award nomination for her role as Rosamund in a Robin Hood retelling based on the 1942 Eudora Welty novella of the same name. Name that musical!

    a. *Where Is The Voice Coming From?*
    b. *The Robber Bridegroom*
    c. *The Ponder Heart*
    d. *Delta Wedding*

25. Which actress originated the role of Diana Morales in *A Chorus Line,* whose experiences at her high-school

performing arts class inspired the character's song "Nothing?"

a. Leland Palmer
b. Priscilla Lopez
c. Diane Langton
d. Rita Moreno

ANSWERS

1. B - Barry Bostwick

2. D - "Mr. Cellophane"

3. True! The costumers complained about the logistics of having to dress different actors in the final costumes every night, and the ending was changed so that the same characters are cast each time.

4. A - Stephanie Mills

5. B - Irene Ryan

6. False! It was a master's thesis created by Carnegie Mellon student John-Michael Tebelak.

7. A - The Gospel of Matthew

8. D - Andrea McArdle

9. B - Fats Waller

10. C - André DeShields

11. A - Ben Vereen

12. False! Tim Rice has said that although he had recently learned that Che Guevara was born in Argentina when he was writing the musical, he never intended for the character to be based on him.

13. D - Pamela Blair

14. B - *The Magic Show*

15. True! It was originally titled "Try It and See" and was to be sung by Scottish singer Lulu.

16. C - The Weismann Theatre

17. D - *Company*

18. B - Sweden

19. D - *Pacific Overtures*

20. A - "By the Sea"

21. B - Patricia Birch

22. D - *All About Eve*

23. A - Glynis Johns

24. B - *The Robber Bridegroom*

25. B - Priscilla Lopez

DID YOU KNOW?

- The musical *Chicago* is based on a play that was written by a reporter named Maurine Dallas Watkins, who actually covered two of the trials for the *Chicago Tribune*. Women in Chicago were rarely convicted of murder since it would mean the death penalty, and the press helped turn some of these women who were acquitted into celebrities. Accused murderer Beulah Annan was the basis for Roxie Hart, and nightclub singer Belva Gaertner was the model for Velma Kelly. Watkins initially refused Bob Fosse's request to purchase the rights to the play, but upon her death, her estate made the sale.

- During the run of *Chicago*, Gwen Verdon, who played Roxie Hart, needed to have surgery on her vocal nodes after accidentally inhaling a feather during the show.

- The original Broadway production of *A Chorus Line* ran for 6,137 performances, which made it the longest-running theatrical production in Broadway history. It held that record until it was surpassed by *Cats* in 1997.

- Ben Vereen won the Tony Award for Best Performance by a Leading Actor in a Musical for portraying the amoral Leading Player in Stephen Schwartz's *Pippin*; when the show was revived on Broadway in 2013, Patina Miller won the Tony Award for Best Performance by a Leading Actress in a Musical for the same role, the only time that has ever happened.

- *The Wiz* was a breakthrough for all-Black musicals on Broadway, along with such other productions as *Purlie* and *Raisin*; these big-budget, large-scale musicals would pave the way for later shows.

- *A Chorus Line* was initially developed from recorded sessions meant to resemble group therapy with Broadway dancers who were rarely featured and typically supportive; some who attended the sessions played the characters that were constructed from their stories, like Priscilla Lopez, who actually attended the High School of Performing Arts.

- In 1973, Bob Fosse became the only person to have won an Oscar (Best Director for *Cabaret*), an Emmy (Outstanding Directorial Achievement for *Liza with a Z*), and a Tony Award (Best Director for *Pippin*) in the same year.

- All five of Stephen Sondheim's musicals that premiered during the 1970s were produced with Hal Prince as director.

- Michael Bennett, who directed and choreographed *A Chorus Line*, and Priscilla Lopez, who originated the role of Diana Morales, met before the taping sessions that led to the show. Lopez was cast in the 1967 production of *Henry, Sweet Henry*, a musical adaptation of the novel *The World of Henry Orient*, which was directed by Michael Bennett and which closed after eighty performances.

- Michael Bennett and Donna McKechnie, who played Cassie, married shortly after winning their respective Tony Awards for *A Chorus Line*, but they separated after only a few months and divorced a few years later.

CHAPTER 6:

THE 1980S

"From the start, it has been the theatre's business to entertain people...it needs no other passport than fun."
- Bertolt Brecht

TRIVIA TIME!

1. True or False: Director-choreographer Gower Champion passed away a few hours before the opening-night curtain of his musical *42nd Street*.

2. Which famous song conveying naive optimism does Joseph sing in the first act of *Joseph and the Amazing Technicolor Dreamcoat*?

   a. "Close Every Door"
   b. "Give Me My Colored Coat"
   c. "Any Dream Will Do"
   d. "Joseph's Dreams"

3. When *Dreamgirls* was produced on Broadway in 1981, its plot was criticized for being too similar to the story of which real-life Motown girl group?

a. The Chiffons
b. The Shirelles
c. Martha and the Vandellas
d. The Supremes

4. Which actress originated the role of Effie Melody White in *Dreamgirls*, for which she won a Tony Award for Best Performance by a Leading Actress in a Musical and two Grammy Awards for the cast album and her awe-inspiring performance of "And I Am Telling You I'm Not Going?"

a. Jennifer Holliday
b. Jennifer Hudson
c. Jennifer Lewis
d. Sharon Brown

5. When Maury Yeston and Tommy Tune began to audition actors for their production of *Nine*, Yeston was so dissatisfied with the men's auditions that the show was rewritten to feature mainly women. Which actor was the exception to Yeston's dislike, who was cast in the lead role of Guido Contini?

a. Emilio Delgado
b. Raul Julia
c. José Ferrer
d. Sergio Franchi

6. Which Brooklyn-born actress was cast as the doe-eyed, hapless Audrey in *Little Shop of Horrors* by Alan Menken and Howard Ashman, a role that she originated off-off-Broadway, played for five years at the Orpheum Theatre off-Broadway, and revisited in the 1986 film adaptation?

a. Denise Kirby

b. Sheila McCarthy

c. Ellen Greene

d. Laurie Beechman

7. The lyrics to Andrew Lloyd Webber's megamusical *Cats* were taken from *Old Possum's Book of Practical Cats*, a 1939 book of poetry from which Nobel Prize-winning writer?

a. Rudyard Kipling

b. William Butler Yeats

c. Hermann Hesse

d. T. S. Eliot

8. Which actor whose Broadway debut was in the 1980 production of *Barnum* played the Rum Tum Tugger in the 1982 Broadway production of *Cats*, where he met and danced alongside his future wife Charlotte d'Amboise?

a. Terrence Mann

b. Paul Nicholas

c. John Partridge

d. David Hibbard

9. True or False: When Arthur Laurents, Harvey Fierstein, and Jerry Herman met together to begin work on *La Cage aux Folles*, they already had the entire plot outlined as well as a basic script.

10. The Pulitzer Prize-winning musical *Sunday in the Park with George* by Stephen Sondheim and James Lapine was inspired by the Pointillist painting *A Sunday Afternoon on the Island of La Grande Jatte* by which French painter?

a. Paul Signac

b. Robert Delaunay

c. Camille Pissarro

d. Georges Seurat

11. Which famous actress of the Broadway stage was nominated for a Tony Award for playing Dot in *Sunday in the Park with George*, her third nomination, but did not win her first Tony Award until 1985 for playing Emma in *Song and Dance* by Andrew Lloyd Webber?

a. Bernadette Peters

b. Sarah Brightman

c. Betty Buckley

d. Maria Friedman

12. Which Country Music Hall of Fame inductee provided the score for *Big River: The Adventures of Huckleberry Finn*, which won him both a Tony Award for Best Original Score and two Drama Desk Awards for Outstanding Music and Outstanding Lyrics in 1985?

a. Merle Travis

b. Hank Snow

c. Roger Miller

d. Marty Robbins

13. True or False: The 1985 production of *The Mystery of Edwin Drood* was the first Broadway musical to feature different endings that would be determined by audience vote.

14. Which Broadway actress won a Tony Award for her portrayal of Grizabella the Glamour Cat in *Cats* and then originated the title role in *The Mystery of Edwin Drood* in 1985?

a. Cleo Laine

b. Betty Buckley

    c. Donna Murphy

    d. Elaine Paige

15. True or False: The only two actors who appeared in both the West End and Broadway productions of *Les Misérables* were Colm Wilkinson, who played Valjean, and Roger Allam, who played Javert.

16. Despite closing after only four performances, this musical received five Tony Award nominations, including one for Best Musical. Which famous 1987 flop featured Teresa Stratas and Larry Kert as Rebecca and Nathan, Judy Kuhn as Bella, and Terrence Mann as Saul?

    a. *Me and My Girl*

    b. *My One and Only*

    c. *Rags*

    d. *Aspects of Love*

17. The 1987 Broadway production of *Into the Woods*, another Sondheim and Lapine collaboration following the success of *Sunday in the Park with George*, integrated several different fairy tales from the Brothers Grimm. Which song sees Cinderella and the Baker comforting Little Red Riding Hood and Jack after each of them has lost someone?

    a. "No One is Alone"

    b. "Ever After"

    c. "Children Will Listen"

    d. "No More"

18. True or False: Andrew Lloyd Webber's adaptation of Gaston Leroux's 1910 novel *The Phantom of the Opera* was the first musical adaptation of that story.

19. The music for the 1988 Broadway musical *Chess*, which uses a chess tournament as a stage for U.S.-Soviet tensions during the Cold War, is written by Benny Andersson and Björn Ulvaeus, who are better associated with which famous pop group?

    a. ABBA
    b. Bee Gees
    c. Blondie
    d. Boney M

20. The 1989 musical *Grand Hotel* is adapted from the 1929 novel as well as the star-studded 1932 film that starred Greta Garbo, John Barrymore, and Joan Crawford. Which young Broadway actress was cast in the Joan Crawford role of the secretary Flaemmchen, which earned her a nomination for a Tony Award?

    a. Lynnette Perry
    b. Yvonne Marceau
    c. Karen Akers
    d. Jane Krakowski

21. Which famous actor of stage and screen earned a Tony Award for his work as Che in *Evita* in 1980 and a nomination for his portrayal of the artist in *Sunday in the Park with George* in 1984?

    a. Mandy Patinkin
    b. Philip Quast
    c. Colm Wilkinson
    d. Gary Bond

ANSWERS

1. True! The cast, including Champion's girlfriend, Wanda Richert, who was playing Peggy Sawyer, were only informed after an enormous standing ovation at the end of the musical.

2. C - "Any Dream Will Do"

3. D - The Supremes

4. A - Jennifer Holliday

5. B - Raul Julia

6. C - Ellen Greene

7. D - T. S. Eliot

8. A - Terrence Mann

9. False! They actually only had the one song "I Am What I Am" that would define the plot and themes of the piece and go on to become a gay anthem.

10. D - Georges Seurat

11. A - Bernadette Peters

12. C - Roger Miller

13. True! The audience votes on who killed Edwin Drood, who could the mysterious

14. Dick Datchery be, and which romantic couple will get together for a happy

15. ending.

16. B - Betty Buckley

17. False! Colm Wilkinson did play Jean Valjean in both roles, but the other actor

18. who starred in both productions was Frances Ruffelle, who played Éponine.

19. C - *Rags*

20. A - "No One is Alone"

21. False! The first musical adaptation of *The Phantom of the Opera* was in 1976

22. with a score by Ken Hill.

23. A - ABBA

24. D - Jane Krakowski

25. A - Mandy Patinkin

DID YOU KNOW?

- The Broadway production of *The Phantom of the Opera* played its 10,000th performance in 2012 and was the first show to do so.

- Andrew Lloyd Webber's 1984 musical *Starlight Express* tells the story of trains, typically played by actors on roller skates; the old steam engine Rusty wants to win a championship race against more modern engines to impress a train named Pearl. Since 1998, it has played without stopping in Bochum, Germany, in a theater that was purpose-built in less than a year.

- *Joseph and the Amazing Technicolor Dreamcoat* was the first collaboration between Andrew Lloyd Webber and Tim Rice to be performed publicly.

- Another Andrew Lloyd Webber musical with its own purpose-built theater is *Cats*, which has played continuously in Tokyo since 1983. Original cast member Yoshiko Hattori played Jennyanydots for twenty years, with over 4,000 performances to her name.

- The original concept album for *Les Misérables* was recorded in French; the English version of the lyrics by Herbert Kretzmer are about one-third rough translation of the French, one-third adapted from the French lyrics, and one-third original material. The famous "To love another person is to see the face of God" was adapted from the original French lyric "Qui aime sa femme, sans le savoir, aime Dieu" or "Who loves his wife, without knowing it, loves God."

- *La Cage aux Folles,* which means "the cage of mad women" or "the cage of effeminate homosexual men" in slang, has won a Best Musical Tony Award for all three of its productions, including two revivals.

- *The Mystery of Edwin Drood* was written by Rupert Holmes, who is perhaps most famous for his recording of "Escape (The Piña Colada Song)."

- During the 1980s, most successful Broadway productions were transfers from the United Kingdom's West End. *Big River* was one of the few American musicals to run for over 1,000 performances during that decade.

- Stephen Sondheim and James Lapine's *Sunday in the Park with George* became the sixth musical ever to be awarded the Pulitzer Prize for Drama in 1985.

- Famous English model and actress Twiggy made her Broadway debut in the musical *My One and Only* alongside director-choreographer Tommy Tune in 1983, for which she received a Tony Award nomination.

CHAPTER 7:

THE 1990S

"Theatre isn't there to provide answers. Only
possibilities. I just ask the questions. But I believe
hope comes from the fact that there is a potential for
redemption. At the core, that's what matters...do we dare
to hope? Do we allow ourselves to hope?" - Joe Mantello

TRIVIA TIME!

1. The main antagonist of the 1990 one-act musical *Once on this Island* is this demon of death, inspired by the Haitian *loa*; in Haitian tradition, he is the corpse of the first man who ever died.

   a. Baron Samedi
   b. Maman Brigitte
   c. Agwe
   d. Papa Ge

2. True or False: *Once on this Island* was the Broadway debut of the music writing team of Lynn Ahrens and Stephen Flaherty.

3. What Puccini opera originally set in Japan was the inspiration for *Miss Saigon*, which takes place in Vietnam during the Vietnam War?

   a. *Tosca*
   b. *Madame Butterfly*
   c. *La rondine*
   d. *Manon Lescaut*

4. Which famous Filipina singer and actress originated the role of Kim in the 1989 West End production of *Miss Saigon*, winning an Olivier Award, and then transferred with the show to Broadway in 1991, winning a Tony Award?

   a. Monique Wilson
   b. Isay Alvarez
   c. Kam Cheng
   d. Lea Salonga

5. True or False: The American Equity Association tried to block Jonathan Pryce from playing a Eurasian pimp in The Engineer in the Broadway transfer of *Miss Saigon*.

6. Which musical adaptation of the Frances Hodgson Burnett novel tells the story of Mary Lennox, an English orphan sent from the British Raj to live in England with a relation she has never met?

   a. *The Secret Garden*
   b. *A Little Princess*
   c. *Little Lord Fauntleroy*
   d. *The Lost Prince*

7. The trio of one-act musicals by William Finn and James Lapine that appeared off-Broadway from 1979 to 1990 was united into one show that premiered on Broadway in 1992. What was this integrated musical named, which won two Tony Awards for Best Book and Best Original Score?

    a. *In Trousers*
    b. *Falsettos*
    c. *March of the Falsettos*
    d. *Falsettoland*

8. What concept album by a British rock band was adapted into a stage production on Broadway in 1993 and tells the story of a pinball prodigy who goes deaf, mute, and blind when he sees his father shoot his mother's new boyfriend?

    a. *The Wall*
    b. *Joe's Garage*
    c. *The Grand Illusion*
    d. *Tommy*

9. True or False: Brent Carver, Anthony Crivello, and Chita Rivera played the roles of Molina, Valentin, and Aurora in each production of *Kiss of the Spider Woman* leading up to and including its 1993 Broadway transfer.

10. Who was the book writer for *Kiss of the Spider Woman* and *Ragtime*, who won four of his five Tony Awards in the 1990s?

    a. George C. Wolfe
    b. Terrence McNally
    c. Peter Stone
    d. Don Black

11. Who composed the score for the 1991 Walt Disney film *Beauty and the Beast* as well as the six additional songs added when the musical was adapted for Broadway in 1994?

    a. Alan Menken
    b. Mark Mancina
    c. Robert B. Sherman
    d. Michael Giacchino

12. True or False: The film's lyricist Howard Ashman provided the lyrics for the new songs added to the *Beauty and the Beast* musical.

13. Which actress received her first Tony Award for portraying the homely and obsessive Fosca in Stephen Sondheim and James Lapine's *Passion* in 1994?

    a. Maria Friedman
    b. Marin Mazzie
    c. Judy Kuhn
    d. Donna Murphy

14. Marin Mazzie received three Tony Award nominations during the 1990s, one for *Passion*, one for the 1999 revival of Cole Porter's *Kiss Me, Kate*, and one for her portrayal of Mother in which musical that chronicled the stories of three families at the turn of the twentieth century?

    a. *Out of This World*
    b. *Ragtime*
    c. *And The World Goes 'Round*
    d. *Where's Charley?*

15. True or False: Glenn Close originated the role of Norma Desmond in the Broadway production of Andrew Lloyd

Webber's stage adaptation of the 1950 Billy Wilder film *Sunset Boulevard.*

16. *RENT* by Jonathan Larson was first performed at the New York Theatre Workshop in 1994, produced on Broadway in 1996, and transferred to the West End in 1998. Which actor played the role of Mark Cohen in each of the three productions?

    a. Adam Pascal
    b. Neil Patrick Harris
    c. Adam Rickett
    d. Anthony Rapp

17. Frank Wildhorn began work on his musical adaptation of *The Strange Case of Dr. Jekyll and Mr. Hyde* in 1990; when the show finally opened on Broadway in 1997, Wildhorn's future wife had played the role of Lucy Harris in each production. Who is this American songstress?

    a. Linda Eder
    b. Colleen Sexton
    c. Carolee Carmello
    d. Rebecca Spencer

18. True or False: The gender of Rafiki was changed to female in the stage production of Walt Disney's *The Lion King.*

19. Though four of the actors from *Ragtime* were nominated for Tony Awards for their performances, this actress was the only winner. Name this actress who won her third Tony Award for her portrayal of Sarah in *Ragtime.*

    a. Camille Saviola
    b. Lynnette Perry

c. Maria Friedman

d. Audra McDonald

20. The second revival of *Gypsy* starred this actress as Mama Rose in her first musical. Which actress won the 1990 Tony Award for Best Performance by a Leading Actress in a Musical?

a. Tyne Daly

b. Angela Lansbury

c. Patti LuPone

d. Bernadette Peters

21. Ten years after his last Tony nomination for *Barnum*, Cy Coleman took home two Tony Awards in 1990 for his score for which musical comedy that paid tribute to the film noir genre?

a. *Aspects of Love*

b. *The Will Rogers Follies*

c. *City of Angels*

d. *Jelly's Last Jam*

ANSWERS

1. D - Papa Ge

2. True! They had produced one musical off-Broadway called *Lucky Stiff* prior to working on *Once on This Island*.

3. B - *Madame Butterfly*

4. D - Lea Salonga

5. True! The AEA's position was that Pryce playing an Asian role was insulting to the Asian community. Cameron Mackintosh threatened to cancel the entire production, and the AEA made a deal to allow Pryce to play The Engineer.

6. A - *The Secret Garden*

7. B - *Falsettos*

8. D - *Tommy*

9. False! The musical was workshopped with an entirely different cast; Carver, Crivello, and Rivera were not cast until the Toronto production in 1992.

10. B - Terrence McNally

11. A - Alan Menken

12. False! Howard Ashman had died in 1991, so the new songs had lyrics written by Tim Rice instead.

13. D - Donna Murphy

14. B - *Ragtime*

15. False! The role was originated on the West End by Patti LuPone, but, in a famous contractual breach, Glenn Close was given the role when it transferred to Broadway.

16. D - Anthony Rapp

17. A - Linda Eder

18. True! The change was made to provide a lead female character in the musical.

19. D - Audra McDonald

20. A - Tyne Daly

21. C - *City of Angels*

DID YOU KNOW?

- In 1991, Lea Salonga won the Tony Award for Best Performance by a Leading Actress in a Musical, making her the first woman of Asian descent to win a Tony Award.

- Lucy Simon, who provided the score for the 1991 musical *The Secret Garden*, is the older sister of musician Carly Simon.

- When Daisy Eagan won the Tony Award for Best Performance by a Featured Actress in a Musical in 1991 at the age of eleven, she became the youngest female ever to win a Tony Award.

- In 1996, *RENT* became the seventh musical to win the Pulitzer Prize for Drama.

- Julie Taymor became the first woman to receive the Tony Award for Best Direction of a Musical for her work on *The Lion King* in 1997. She also received the Tony Award that year for her costume design, which integrated large masks.

- *RENT* is considered to be one of the most culturally significant musicals of all time by some, but its writer would never see any of that acclaim. Jonathan Larson, who wrote the music, lyrics, and book, died unexpectedly from an aortic dissection on the morning of *RENT*'s first preview performance off-Broadway. He would receive three posthumous Tony Awards as well as his posthumous Pulitzer.

- In 1999, Frank Wildhorn joined the select ranks of composers who have had three shows playing on Broadway at once: *Jekyll and Hyde*, *The Scarlet Pimpernel*, and *The Civil War*. None of the shows recouped their initial investment.

- Audra McDonald is one of only four actors to have won three Tony Awards within five years for productions of *Carousel*, *Master Class*, and *Ragtime*; the other three are Zero Mostel, Shirley Booth, and Gwen Verdon.

- Despite running for over two years on Broadway, *Sunset Boulevard* holds the record for the most money lost by a theatrical production in United States history.

- *The Lion King* holds the record for the highest-earning title for both stage productions and film in box-office history.

CHAPTER 8:

THE 2000S

*"Theatre is a verb before it is a noun, an act
before it is a place." - Martha Graham*

TRIVIA TIME!

1. What Italian opera composer's work *Aida* that tells of the
   tragic love story between the Ethiopian princess Aida and
   the Egyptian general Radames was adapted into a musical
   by Elton John and Tim Rice?

   a. Giuseppe Verdi
   b. Gioachino Rossini
   c. Vincenzo Bellini
   d. Giovanni Pacini

2. Who replaced Kathleen Freeman as Jeanette Burmeister in
   the Broadway production of *The Full Monty* when she was
   forced to leave the show due to her worsening lung
   cancer?

   a. Elaine Stritch
   b. Jane Connell

   c. Madeline Kahn

   d. Carol Burnett

3. True or False: Though the 2001 Broadway production of *The Producers* was directed and choreographed by Susan Stroman, it was originally her husband Mike Ockrent who had been tapped to direct.

4. True or False: After the attacks on 9/11, *Urinetown* had to postpone its opening night in order to cut the script of anything that would have been considered offensive in the light of the recent tragedy.

5. Which of ABBA's songs inspired producer Judy Craymer to commission a book writer for a new jukebox musical based on their discography?

   a. "Mamma Mia"

   b. "The Name of the Game"

   c. "The Winner Takes It All"

   d. "S.O.S."

6. Which composer joined forces with lyricist Dick Scanlan to write new music for a stage adaptation of *Thoroughly Modern Millie*, which led to her first nomination for the Tony Award for Best Original Score?

   a. Mindi Dickstein

   b. Marsha Norman

   c. Nell Benjamin

   d. Jeanine Tesori

7. Which contemporary Broadway composer, whose musical *The Light in the Piazza* earned him two Tony Awards, one for Best Original Score and one for Best Orchestrations, is actually the grandson of Richard Rodgers?

a. Adam Guettel
b. David Yazbek
c. Tom Kitt
d. Michael John LaChiusa

8. The hugely popular 2008 musical *In the Heights* takes place over three days in which neighborhood of Manhattan?

a. Spanish Harlem
b. Morningside Heights
c. Washington Heights
d. Marble Hill

9. This energetic final number from 2002's *Hairspray* pays homage to Ike and Tina Turner's "River Deep—Mountain High" and proclaims that change and progress cannot be hindered by those who cling to hatred and tradition. What's the name of this song, lauded by some critics as the perfect ending number?

a. "Without Love"
b. "You Can't Stop the Beat"
c. "Run and Tell That!"
d. "Welcome to the 60's"

10. The 2002 Billy Joel jukebox-musical *Movin' Out* was directed and choreographed by which legend of American contemporary ballet who received the Tony Award for Best Choreography that year?

a. Kathleen Marshall
b. Susan Stroman
c. Jerry Mitchell
d. Twyla Tharp

11. True or False: The role of Gary Coleman in *Avenue Q* was offered to Gary Coleman himself.

12. True or False: Idina Menzel played the role of Elphaba in *Wicked*'s developmental workshops.

13. Which 2009 rock musical by Brian Yorkey and Tom Kitt explored Diana Goodman's worsening bipolar disorder and its effects on her husband Dan and daughter Natalie?

    a. *Next to Normal*
    b. *Feeling Electric*
    c. *Everyday Rapture*
    d. *If/Then*

14. Which German playwright wrote *Spring Awakening*, the play that inspired the 2006 Broadway musical adaptation of the same name?

    a. Carl Sternheim
    b. Ernst Hardt
    c. Georg Kaiser
    d. Frank Wedekind

15. What was the name of the original improvisational play that inspired the musical *The 25th Annual Putnam County Spelling Bee*?

    a. *V-I-V-I-S-E-P-U-L-T-U-R-E*
    b. *C-R-E-P-U-S-C-U-L-E*
    c. *S-U-C-C-E-D-A-N-E-U-M*
    d. *K-N-A-I-D-E-L*

16. True or False: The writers of *Jersey Boys* were contacted by family members of the deceased mob boss Gyp DeCarlo

who wanted to ensure that he was portrayed respectfully in the musical.

17. The silly musical-within-a-musical *The Drowsy Chaperone* earned this triple threat her third Tony Award nomination for playing Janet van de Graaff, a leading lady of *Feldzieg's Follies* who is leaving show business to get married but can't resist an encore or a chance to show off. Who is this Broadway actress, who had previously received Tony nominations for Millie Dillmount and Jo March?

    a. Sutton Foster
    b. Kate Fisher
    c. Mara Davi
    d. Jenn Robertson

18. The 2005 musical adaptation of *Dirty Rotten Scoundrels* was nominated for ten Tony Awards, but only won one: Best Performance by a Leading Actor in a Musical. Which Broadway actor won the Tony Award for his portrayal of con-artist Freddy Benson?

    a. John Lithgow
    b. Brian d'Arcy James
    c. Jonathan Pryce
    d. Norbert Leo Butz

19. True or False: Broadway singer and actor Matthew Morrison was part of an early-2000s boy band.

20. Which actor played the role of common-law assistant Carmen Ghia in the 2001 Broadway adaptation of *The Producers*, a role which he reprised in the 2005 film adaptation?

a. Matthew Broderick
b. Roger Bart
c. Gary Beach
d. James Dreyfus

ANSWERS

1. A - Giuseppe Verdi

2. B - Jane Connell

3. True! Mike Ockrent was persuaded by Mel Brooks to direct, but after his death, Stroman took over both aspects of the musical.

4. False! Opening night was delayed, but it wasn't due to the script needing major edits. Only one line from the show was replaced.

5. C - "The Winner Takes It All"

6. D - Jeanine Tesori

7. A - Adam Guettel

8. C - Washington Heights

9. B - "You Can't Stop the Beat"

10. D - Twyla Tharp

11. True! He reportedly never showed up for the meeting where the writing team

12. would pitch the idea to him.

13. False! Stephanie J. Block, who would go on to play Elphaba in the first national

14. tour, played Elphaba during the workshop phase.

15. A - *Next to Normal*

16. D - Frank Wedekind

17. B - *C-R-E-P-U-S-C-U-L-E*

18. True! Since the writers never turned up with cement blocks on their feet, the

19. family must have liked it.

20. A - Sutton Foster

21. D - Norbert Leo Butz

22. True! Morrison was part of the band LMNT but was replaced within a year.

23. B - Roger Bart

DID YOU KNOW?

- When Susan Stroman won the Tony Award for Best Direction of a Musical for *The Producers* in 2001, she became the second woman to win the award. When she won the Tony Award for Best Choreography that night, she became the only woman to win both awards on the same night.

- The first national tour of *In the Heights* in 2009 was the first Equity tour to play in San Juan, Puerto Rico.

- None of the dancers in Twyla Tharp's *Movin' Out* sang. Instead, the music was performed by a pianist and band on a platform suspended above the stage, which has led to the show being categorized as a rock ballet.

- *In the Heights* has been produced all over the world, including in South Korea. The 2015 Seoul production featured numerous K-pop idols, including Key from Shinee as Usnavi, Chen from EXO as Benny, and Luna from f(x) as Nina.

- One of the leitmotifs used in the score for *Wicked*, referred to by Stephen Schwartz as the "unlimited theme," uses the first seven notes of "Over the Rainbow" as a tribute to its composer Harold Arlen.

- *Next to Normal* made history as only the eighth musical to have been awarded the Pulitzer Prize for Drama in 2010.

- The Broadway production of *Wicked* has broken the house record at the Gershwin Theatre twenty times since the show's opening in 2003.

- William Finn's *25th Annual Putnam County Spelling Bee* uses audience participation by having volunteer spellers from the crowd who join the actors onstage and wait their turn to try and spell a word correctly or be eliminated. In 2007, Dame Julie Andrews misspelled supercalifragilisticexpialidocious.

- In 2001, *The Producers* was nominated for fifteen Tony Awards. It won twelve out of the fifteen, setting a record and winning for every category in which it was nominated.

- The musical adaptation of *Billy Elliot*, with a score composed by Elton John, required three young actors to cover the role of Billy for all eight shows a week. All three actors were nominated for the Tony Award for Best Performance by a Leading Actor in a Musical, and the win marked the first time the award had been awarded to three actors.

CHAPTER 9:

THE 2010S

"The good die young but not always. The wicked prevail but not consistently. I am confused by life, and I feel safe within the confines of the theatre." - Helen Hayes

TRIVIA TIME!

1. Which Green Day album was adapted into a flashy Broadway musical that won two Tony Awards in 2010, one for Best Scenic Design of a Musical and one for Best Lighting Design of a Musical?

    a. *Nimrod*

    b. *Dookie*

    c. *21st Century Breakdown*

    d. *American Idiot*

2. What city does the virtuous Elder Price pray to be sent to in order to complete his two-year mission at the beginning of Trey Parker and Matt Stone's hilarious 2011 musical *The Book of Mormon*?

    a. Salt Lake City

    b. Orlando

c. San Francisco

d. Tokyo

3. Who finished the lyrics for the 2010 musical *The Scottsboro Boys* after the death of Fred Ebb in 2004?

a. John Kander

b. Glenn Slater

c. Brian Yorkey

d. Michael Korie

4. Which English theatre director, former Associate Director of New Work at the National Theatre of Scotland, won a Tony Award for Best Direction of a Musical for the 2012 stage adaptation of the Irish romantic drama *Once*?

a. Bill T. Jones

b. Terry Johnson

c. Sam Gold

d. John Tiffany

5. True or False: The 2012 Gershwin musical *Nice Work If You Can Get It* was originally titled *They All Laughed!*

6. Christopher Gattelli's Broadway career began in 2006 with *Martin Short: Fame Becomes Me,* and he has since been nominated for the Tony Award for Best Choreography twice. Which toe-tapping musical did Gattelli win the Tony Award for in 2012?

a. *Newsies*

b. *Leap of Faith*

c. *Sister Act*

d. *Bring It On: The Musical*

7. *Kinky Boots*, based on the 2005 film, tells the story of shoe factory heir Charlie and his unlikely partnership with drag queen Lola. What famous 1980s pop singer wrote the music for the 2012 stage adaptation which earned her a Tony Award for Best Original Score?

    a. Kate Bush
    b. Madonna
    c. Cyndi Lauper
    d. Cher

8. The book for *Matilda the Musical* may have been written by Tim Minchin, but which children's author wrote the 1988 novel?

    a. A. Milne
    b. Philip Pullman
    c. Lewis Caroll
    d. Roald Dahl

9. Which actor originated the role of The D'Ysquith Family — which comprises Lord Adalbert, Lord Henry, Lord Asquith, Asquith Jr., the Reverend Ezekiel, Major Lord Bartholomew, Lady Salome, Lady Hyacinth, and Chauncey — in the 2013 production of *A Gentleman's Guide to Love and Murder*?

    a. Jefferson Mays
    b. Bertie Carvel
    c. Rob McClure
    d. Michael Cerveris

10. True or False: The 2015 Broadway production of *Fun Home* marked the first Broadway musical with a lesbian protagonist.

11. The 2015 musical play *An American in Paris* was adapted from the 1951 Gene Kelly film that was based on the orchestral compositions of what famous American composer?

    a. Leonard Bernstein
    b. Aaron Copland
    c. George Gershwin
    d. Cole Porter

12. Who wrote the 2004 biography of Alexander Hamilton that composer and lyricist Lin-Manuel Miranda read while on vacation from performing in his musical *In the Heights* that inspired him to write *Hamilton*?

    a. Jon Meacham
    b. Ron Chernow
    c. Niall Ferguson
    d. David Herbert Donald

13. Which American singer-songwriter of songs like "Brave" and "Love Song" provided the score to the 2016 Broadway adaptation of *Waitress* which earned her a Tony nomination? She would go on to play the role of Jenna later in the show's run.

    a. Sara Bareilles
    b. Katharine McPhee
    c. Lady Gaga
    d. Ingrid Michaelson

14. True or False: The 2016 Broadway production of *Shuffle Along, or, the Making of the Musical Sensation of 1921 and All That Followed* is considered a revival.

15. Which composer-lyricist team that wrote "City of Stars" from *La La Land* and "This Is Me" from *The Greatest Showman* won their first Tony Award for Best Original Score with the 2016 Broadway production *Dear Evan Hansen*?

   a. Robert Lopez and Kristen Anderson-Lopez
   b. Jeanine Tesori and Lisa Kron
   c. Duncan Sheik and Steven Sater
   d. Benj Pasek and Justin Paul

16. This 2017 Broadway musical was based on the September 11 attacks and the planes that were rerouted to an island called Gander in Newfoundland, Canada. Which musical told the stories of the town's residents, as well as the almost 7000 displaced travelers, and earned Christopher Ashley a Tony Award for Best Direction of a Musical?

   a. *Bright Star*
   b. *Come From Away*
   c. *The Visit*
   d. *Something Rotten!*

17. The electro-pop opera *Natasha, Pierre, and the Great Comet of 1812* is a sung-through musical adaptation of a seventy-page section from what famous Russian novel?

   a. *Anna Karenina*
   b. *Crime and Punishment*
   c. *War and Peace*
   d. *The Brothers Karamazov*

18. *The Band's Visit*, a musical adaptation of the 2007 Israeli film, was composed by which contemporary American

composer, who also composed *The Full Monty, Dirty Rotten Scoundrels,* and *Women on the Verge of a Nervous Breakdown?*

    a. David Yazbek

    b. Michael John LaChiusa

    c. Andrew Lippa

    d. Matthew Sklar

19. True or False: David Bowie composed a song for the 2017 Broadway musical *SpongeBob SquarePants.*

20. Which famous pair of lovers have their story told in *Hadestown,* Anais Mitchell's American folk retelling of the tragic Greek myth?

    a. Eros and Psyche

    b. Perseus and Andromeda

    c. Jason and Medea

    d. Orpheus and Eurydice

ANSWERS

1. D - *American Idiot*

2. B - Orlando

3. A - John Kander

4. D - John Tiffany

5. True! The musical was originally a different Gershwin tribute musical entirely that premiered in 2001 to mediocre reviews.

6. A - *Newsies*

7. C - Cyndi Lauper

8. D - Roald Dahl

9. A - Jefferson Mays

10. True! Broadway plays had featured lesbians as leads before, but *Fun Home*

11. marked the first for a musical.

12. C - George Gershwin

13. B - Ron Chernow

14. A - Sara Bareilles

15. False! Since it includes new material surrounding the difficulties of mounting the

16. original production, the show was considered a new musical.

17. D - Benj Pasek and Justin Paul

18. B - *Come From Away*

19. C - *War and Peace*

20. A - David Yazbek

21. True! "No Control" is sung by the town of Bikini Bottom in the face of a volcano

22. that may soon erupt.

23. D - Orpheus and Eurydice

DID YOU KNOW?

- In 2011, choreographer Sergio Trujillo had four shows featuring his work running on Broadway: *Memphis*, *Jersey Boys*, *The Addams Family*, and *Next to Normal*.

- Green Day front man Billie Joe Armstrong joined the Broadway cast of *American Idiot* onstage in 2010 when he performed the role of St. Jimmy, a drug dealer who is revealed to be Johnny's alter ego, for a few separate weeks of the show's run.

- *Matilda the Musical* performed well at the 2013 Tony Awards, but its 2012 West End production set a record by receiving seven Olivier Awards, the most ever won by a single show.

- When Cyndi Lauper won her Tony Award for Best Original Score for *Kinky Boots* in 2013, she made history as the first woman to win alone in that category.

- *Hamilton* broke the record previously held by *The Producers* when it received sixteen Tony Award nominations in 2016.

- The original Broadway cast recording of *The Book of Mormon* reached spot number three on the *Billboard* charts in 2011, which made it the highest-charting Broadway cast album in over forty years.

- In 2015, Jeanine Tesori and Lisa Kron became the first female writing team to win the Tony Award for Best Original Score for *Fun Home*.

- The 2010 Broadway production of *The Scottsboro Boys* set a record when it was nominated for twelve Tony Awards but received none.

- *Hamilton* became the ninth musical to win the Pulitzer Prize for Drama in 2016.

- *The Band's Visit* is one of only four musicals in history to win the Big Six Tony Awards — Best Musical, Best Book, Best Original Score, Best Performance by a Leading Actor in a Musical, Best Performance by a Leading Actress in a Musical, and Best Direction of a Musical — which it did in 2018.

CHAPTER 10:

DAMES AND DIVAS

"In almost every musical ever written, there's a place that's usually about the third song of the evening - sometimes it's the second, sometimes it's the fourth, but it's quite early - and the leading lady usually sits down on something; sometimes it's a tree stump in Brigadoon, sometimes it's under the pillars of Covent Garden in My Fair Lady, or it's a trash can in Little Shop of Horrors... but the leading lady sits down on something and sings about what she wants in life. And the audience falls in love with her and then roots for her to get it for the rest of the night." - Howard Ashman

TRIVIA TIME!

Name the great legend of the Broadway stage based on their association with these standards:

1. "I Got Rhythm," "Everything's Coming Up Roses," "There's No Business Like Show Business," "It's De-Lovely"

   a. Rosalind Russell
   b. Dolores Gray

c. Gertrude Lawrence

d. Ethel Merman ✓

2. "Don't Cry for Me Argentina," "The Ladies Who Lunch," "Rose's Turn," "Meadowlark"

a. Elaine Paige

b. Madeline Kahn

c. Patti LuPone

d. Glenn Close

3. "We Need a Little Christmas," "Beauty and the Beast," "The Worst Pies in London," "The Age of Not Believing"

a. Carol Channing

b. Angela Lansbury

c. Bea Arthur

d. Glynis Johns

4. "If My Friends Could See Me Now," "Nowadays," "Whatever Lola Wants," "Roxie"

a. Leland Palmer

b. Gwen Verdon ✓

c. Ann Reinking

d. Donna McKechnie

5. "Unexpected Song," "Anything You Can Do," "Children Will Listen," "Losing My Mind"

a. Dorothy Loudon

b. Dorothy Collins

c. Joanna Gleason

d. Bernadette Peters

6. "But the World Goes 'Round," "New York, New York," "Maybe This Time," "Mein Herr"

a. Liza Minnelli ✓
b. Chita Rivera
c. Charlotte d'Amboise
d. Rita Moreno

7. "My Favorite Things," "I Could Have Danced All Night," "Le Jazz Hot," "Do-Re-Mi"

   a. Carol Burnett
   b. Julie Andrews
   c. Audrey Hepburn
   d. Rosalind Russell

8. "Your Daddy's Son," "Climb Ev'ry Mountain," "God Bless the Child," "Stars and the Moon"

   a. Heather Headley
   b. Vanessa Williams
   c. Jennifer Holliday
   d. Audra McDonald

9. "I Won't Grow Up," "I'm Gonna Wash That Man Right Outa My Hair," "My Heart Belongs to Daddy," "A Cockeyed Optimist"

   a. Mary Martin ✓
   b. Grace Hartman
   c. Nanette Fabray
   d. Gertrude Lawrence

10. "Spanish Rose," "All That Jazz," "America," "Kiss of the Spider Woman"

    a. Luba Lisa
    b. Jenny Logan
    c. Eydie Gormé
    d. Chita Rivera ✓

11. "Don't Rain on My Parade," "Somewhere," "People," "Papa, Can You Hear Me?"

    a. Carol Channing

    b. Barbra Streisand

    c. Inga Swenson

    d. Barbara Harris

12. "I Put My Hand In," "Diamonds Are a Girl's Best Friend," "Put On Your Sunday Clothes," "Hello, Dolly!"

    a. Carol Burnett

    b. Elaine Stritch

    c. Debbie Reynolds

    d. Carol Channing ✓

13. "The Ladies Who Lunch," "I'm Still Here," "Broadway Baby," "Pal Joey"

    a. Elaine Stritch ✓

    b. Bernadette Peters

    c. Betty Buckley

    d. Gertrude Lawrence

14. "Vanilla Ice Cream," "Glitter and Be Gay," "My White Knight," "Goodnight My Someone"

    a. Madeline Kahn

    b. Kristin Chenoweth

    c. Patricia Lambert

    d. Barbara Cook ✓

15. "My New Philosophy," "Popular," "Taylor the Latte Boy," "Glitter and Be Gay"

    a. Laura Benanti

    b. Kristin Chenoweth

c. Sutton Foster

d. Laura Osnes

16. "Memory," "He Plays the Violin," "Over You," "When There's No One"

    a. Donna McKechnie

    b. Liz Callaway

    c. Laurie Beechman

    d. Betty Buckley ✓

17. "Someone to Watch Over Me," "The Light in the Piazza," "A Cockeyed Optimist," "Always Better"

    a. Kelli O'Hara ✓

    b. Christine Ebersole

    c. Kerry Butler

    d. Kate Baldwin

18. "Defying Gravity," "Always Starting Over," "The Life of the Party," "Take Me or Leave Me"

    a. Sherie Rene Scott

    b. Eden Espinosa

    c. Idina Menzel

    d. Ashley Williams

19. "Loving You," "One Hundred Easy Ways," "Mother Knows Best," "Shall I Tell You What I Think Of You?"

    a. Victoria Clark

    b. Laura Benanti

    c. Lea Salonga

    d. Donna Murphy ✓

20. "Astonishing," "I Know It's Today," "Gimme Gimme," "Anything Goes"

    a. Kelli O'Hara
    b. Sutton Foster ✓
    c. Stephanie J. Block
    d. Anne L. Nathan

21. "She Used to Be Mine," "Beautiful," "Mister Snow," "If I Loved You"

    a. Sara Bareilles ✓
    b. Audra McDonald
    c. Jessie Mueller
    d. Chilina Kennedy

ANSWERS

1. D - Ethel Merman

2. C - Patti LuPone

3. B - Angela Lansbury

4. B - Gwen Verdon

5. D - Bernadette Peters

6. A - Liza Minnelli

7. B - Julie Andrews

8. D - Audra McDonald

9. A - Mary Martin

10. D - Chita Rivera

11. B - Barbra Streisand

12. D - Carol Channing

13. A - Elaine Stritch

14. D - Barbara Cook

15. B - Kristin Chenoweth

16. D - Betty Buckley

17. A - Kelli O'Hara

18. C - Idina Menzel

19. D - Donna Murphy

20. B - Sutton Foster

21. A - Sara Bareilles

DID YOU KNOW?

- Three-time Tony-nominee Stephanie J. Block was the original Belle in the Disneyland production of *Beauty and the Beast.*

- Lea Salonga, known for her voice work as the singing voices of Princess Jasmine and Mulan in the Disney movie musicals, was the first actress of Asian descent to play the roles of Éponine and Fantine in the Broadway production of *Les Misérables.*

- Judy Kuhn has four Tony Award nominations, but she is perhaps best known for voicing the singing voice of Pocahontas in the 1995 Disney film.

- Laura Benanti got her Broadway start at a very young age! At eighteen, she was cast to understudy Rebecca Luker as Maria in *The Sound of Music.* She had been enrolled at New York University for two weeks when she was cast, and the dean recommended that she go on leave to do the show.

- Carol Burnett was able to go to New York to try musical comedy because of a mysterious benefactor. During her junior year of college at UCLA, she was invited by her professor to perform at a black-tie event. She was approached afterward while she was stuffing cookies into her purse by a man who asked her about her ambitions and promised her a $1000 interest-free loan to go to New York City if she repaid it within five years and never mentioned his name to anyone. She took him up on his offer, and the rest is history!

- Tonya Pinkins may be best known for her soap-opera career, but she has two Tony Award nominations and a Tony Award for her performance as Sweet Anita in *Jelly's Last Jam*.

- Christine Ebersole's first professional theatrical role was in the chorus of *Going Hollywood* in 1983 with future director and choreographer Jerry Mitchell.

- Though Effie White was the role that made her career, Jennifer Holliday has stated that her 2012 performance at the St. Louis Municipal Opera Theatre was the last time she would return to the role.

- The 1969 production of *The Fig Leaves Are Falling* only ran for four performances, but that was long enough for Dorothy Loudon to secure both a Drama Desk Award for Outstanding Performance and her first Tony nomination.

- Jan Maxwell is only the second actress to receive a Tony Award nomination in all four acting categories, and her nominations in two separate categories in 2010 made her the fourth actress to achieve two nominations in a single year.

CHAPTER 11:

THE AWARDS

"Tony, Tony, Tony, Tony, Tony!" - The Producers

TRIVIA TIME!

1. What year was the first Tony Awards ceremony held?

    a. 1945
    b. 1945
    c. 1946
    d. 1947

2. What year was the famous Tony medallion, designed by Herman Rosse, first presented at the Tony Awards ceremony?

    a. 1947
    b. 1948
    c. 1949
    d. 1950

3. Which Broadway musical recently overturned the record for Tony nominations, garnering sixteen during the 2016 awards season?

a. *Hadestown*
b. *Hamilton*
c. *Waitress*
d. *Billy Elliot*

4. Though it no longer holds the record for Tony nominations, which Broadway musical adapted from the 1967 Mel Brooks film still holds the record for most Tony Awards won by a single production?

a. *Young Frankenstein*
b. *Blazing Saddles*
c. *A Gentleman's Guide to Love and Murder*
d. *The Producers*

5. True or False: The record for most-nominated musicals with the fewest wins is shared by two musicals that were both nominated for twelve Tony Awards and won none.

6. Which of these Broadway musicals did not win the Big Six awards (Best Musical, Best Original Score, Best Book of a Musical, Best Performance by a Leading Actor in a Musical, Best Performance by a Leading Actress in a Musical, and Best Direction of a Musical) for their category?

a. *Sweeney Todd: The Demon Barber of Fleet Street*
b. *Hairspray*
c. *The Band's Visit*
d. *The Sound of Music*

7. Theatre is about collaboration, a fact shown very clearly in that only six musicals have won Best Musical when the book and score were written or co-written by the same person. Which musical was the first to achieve this honor?

a. *The Music Man*

b. *The Mystery of Edwin Drood*

c. *RENT*

d. *South Pacific*

8. The glamour and glitz of Broadway would be significantly diminished if it were not for the designers who created the technical elements. Which musical is the first to be considered to have swept the design awards at the Tonys, winning Best Scenic Design of a Musical, Best Costume Design of a Musical, and Best Lighting Design of a Musical, though not Best Sound Design of a Musical, which was added to the awards ceremony in 2008?

a. *The Lion King*

b. *The Phantom of the Opera*

c. *Follies*

d. *Peter Pan*

9. *La Cage aux Folles* made history as the first musical to win Best Production three separate times, but the feat was accomplished in 2015 by which musical that won Best Revival of a Musical that year?

a. *On the Town*

b. *The King and I*

c. *On the Twentieth Century*

d. *Side Show*

10. How many Tony Awards have been awarded to theatre giant Hal Prince, who holds the record for the most Tony Awards won?

a. 18

b. 19

c. 20

d. 21

11. Which prolific composer holds the record for more music Tony Awards won than anyone else?

    a. Richard Rodgers
    b. Stephen Sondheim
    c. Tim Rice
    d. Andrew Lloyd Webber

12. Which iconic choreographer has eight Tony Awards for choreography to his name, the current record?

    a. Bob Fosse
    b. Jerome Robbins
    c. Jack Cole
    d. Gower Champion

13. Which great songstress holds the record for Tony Awards won for performances, with a whopping six?

    a. Patti LuPone
    b. Bernadette Peters
    c. Audra McDonald
    d. Betty Buckley

14. Tom Stoppard has won four writing Tony Awards. Which playwright does he share the record with, who has won Best Book of a Musical twice?

    a. Hugh Wheeler
    b. Terrence McNally
    c. James Lapine
    d. Peter Stone

15. True or False: The record for the most Tony nominations by a performer belongs to Kelli O'Hara.

16. Only five performers have been nominated for Tony Awards in each acting category: Best Performance by a Leading Actor/Actress in a Musical, Best Performance by a Featured Actor/Actress in a Musical, Best Performance by a Leading Actor/Actress in a Play, Best Performance by a Featured Actor/Actress in a Play. Who was the first?

    a. Angela Lansbury
    b. Boyd Gaines
    c. Jan Maxwell
    d. Raúl Esparza

17. Harvey Fierstein has won Tony Awards as both an author and a performer. His two writing Tony Awards were for the plays *Torch Song Trilogy* and *La Cage Aux Folles*; Which musical won him the Best Lead Actor in a Musical Tony Award?

    a. *La Cage aux Folles*
    b. *Little Shop of Horrors*
    c. *Disney's The Little Mermaid*
    d. *Hairspray*

18. True or False: Lin-Manuel Miranda became the youngest composer ever to win a Tony Award when he won Best Original Score for writing *Hamilton* at the age of 36.

19. Only twice has the Tony Award for Best Original Score been awarded posthumously. It was awarded to Jonathan Larson for *RENT* and which perhaps unconventional composer?

111

a. Rupert Holmes

b. T. S. Eliot

c. Roger Miller

d. Kurt Weill

20. Which actress, dancer, and composer became the first woman to win the Tony Award for Best Score?

a. Betty Comden

b. Lynn Ahrens

c. Dorothy Fields

d. Carol Hall

ANSWERS

1. D - 1947

2. C - 1949

3. B - *Hamilton*

4. D - *The Producers*

5. True! *Mean Girls* and *The Scottsboro Boys* share the record.

6. D - *The Sound of Music*

7. A - *The Music Man*

8. C - *Follies*

9. B - *The King and I*

10. D - 21

11. B - Stephen Sondheim

12. A - Bob Fosse

13. C - Audra McDonald

14. B - Terrence McNally

15. False! That record is actually held in a tie between Chita Rivera and Julie Harris

16. with ten nominations each.

17. B - Boyd Gaines

18. D - *Hairspray*

19. False! Lin-Manuel Miranda is the youngest composer to win a Tony Award, but it

20. was won for *In the Heights* when he was 28.

21. B - T. S. Eliot

22. A - Betty Comden

DID YOU KNOW?

- The first Black woman to win the Tony Award for Best Performance by a Featured Actress in a Musical was Juanita Hall, who won in 1950 for her performance as Bloody Mary in *South Pacific*.

- The first person who uses a wheelchair to be nominated for and win a performance Tony Award was Ali Stroker, who won the Tony Award for Best Featured Actress in a Musical for her turn as Ado Annie in the 2019 revival of *Oklahoma!*

- The first Black man to win the Tony Award for Best Performance by a Featured Actor in a Musical was "King of Calypso" Harry Belafonte for the 1954 musical revue *John Murray Anderson's Almanac* which featured the music of Richard Adler and Jerry Ross.

- The 2018 production *The Band's Visit* saw two of its stars set records: Tony Shalhoub became the first Lebanese-American to win the Tony Award for Best Performance by a Leading Actor in a Musical for his role as Tewfiq Zakaria, and Ari'el Stachel became the first Yemeni-American to win the Tony Award for Best Performance by a Featured Actor in a Musical for his role as Haled.

- The first Black woman to win the Tony Award for Best Performance by a Leading Actress in a Musical was Diahann Carroll, who won in 1962 for the role of Barbara Woodruff in *No Strings*, the only musical with both music and lyrics by Richard Rodgers and the first written after the death of his writing partner Oscar Hammerstein II.

- The first Asian-American woman to win the Tony Award for Best Performance by a Featured Actress in a Musical was Korean-American actress Ruthie Ann Miles, who took home the Tony for her performance as Lady Thiang in the 2015 revival of *The King and I*.

- The first Black man to win the Tony Award for Best Performance by a Leading Actor in a Musical was Cleavon Little, famous for his film performance as Sheriff Bart in the 1974 Mel Brooks film *Blazing Saddles*, for his role as traveling preacher Purlie Victorious Judson in the 1970 musical *Purlie*.

- There have only been ten ties in Tony Award history. One of the most famous is the 1960 Best Musical tie between Rodgers and Hammerstein's *The Sound of Music* and Bock and Harnick's *Fiorello!*

- The theater that has housed the most Tony-winning Best Plays and Best Musicals is the Richard Rodgers, located on West 46th St, which has housed eleven.

CHAPTER 12:

MOVIE MUSICALS

"We didn't have a lot of live theatre in Oklahoma. I didn't visit New York when I was growing up. I watched movie musicals, and I believed in an idealistic, idyllic version of Broadway." - Kelli O'Hara

TRIVIA TIME!

1. *Mary Poppins'* 2006 Broadway adaptation combines elements of the original Disney film and the children's books by P. L. Travers that the Disney film is itself based on. Which actress originated the role of Mary Poppins on Broadway?

   a. Laura Michelle Kelly
   b. Ashley Brown
   c. Caroline Sheen
   d. Megan McGinnis

2. True or False: Cloris Leachman, who played Frau Blucher in the movie *Young Frankenstein*, originated the role on Broadway as well.

3. This 2011 musical, which is based on the 2002 film, earned a Tony Award for Norbert Leo Butz, who originated the role of Carl Hanratty, but not Aaron Tveit, who originated the role of con man Frank Abagnale, Jr.

   a. *Dirty Rotten Scoundrels*
   b. *How to Succeed in Business Without Really Trying*
   c. *Catch Me If You Can*
   d. *Sister Act*

4. The 2008 musical *9 to 5* is based on the 1980 film of the same name and tells the story of three women who work in an office: Violet, who is frequently passed over for promotions, Judy, the new girl who has no prior work experience, and Doralee, the object of her boss's leering who thinks of herself as just a pretty face. The role of Doralee was played in the 1980 film by which singer who also wrote the score for the musical?

   a. Linda Ronstadt
   b. Rosanne Cash
   c. Anne Murray
   d. Dolly Parton

5. Which high-belting Broadway actress originated the role of Elle Woods in the 2007 musical adaptation of the 2001 film *Legally Blonde*?

   a. Laura Bell Bundy
   b. Bailey Hanks
   c. Annaleigh Ashford
   d. Becky Gulsvig

6. In the 2008 stage adaptation of the 1989 Disney film *The Little Mermaid*, what kind of shoe was used to create the illusion of gliding through water?

   a. Roller skates
   b. Rollerblades
   c. Pointe shoes
   d. Heelys

7. The role of Donkey in the 2008 stage adaptation *Shrek the Musical* was originated on Broadway by Daniel Breaker, but who was the original actor cast in the show's Seattle premiere, who had previously made his Broadway debut as Seaweed J. Stubbs in *Hairspray*?

   a. Chester Gregory II
   b. Corey Reynolds
   c. Corbin Bleu
   d. Tevin Campbell

8. The book and lyrics for *Billy Elliot the Musical*, which transferred from the West End to Broadway in 2008, were written by Lee Hall, who wrote the screenplay for the 2000 film. Which composer wrote the music?

   a. David Yazbek
   b. Alan Menken
   c. Marc Shaiman
   d. Elton John

9. True or False: The actors cast in the 2014 Broadway adaptation of the Disney animated musical film *Aladdin* were all Middle Eastern.

10. The 2002 stage adaptation of the hit film *Hairspray* featured a score from Marc Shaiman and Scott Wittman and was directed by Jack O'Brien, but who directed the 1988 film?

    a. John Waters
    b. Roger Corman
    c. Douglas Heyes
    d. Rainer Werner Fassbinder

11. While the 2018 Broadway stage adaptation of Disney's *Frozen* opened to mixed reviews and won none of the three Tony Awards for which it was nominated, Michael Curry did win a Drama Desk Award for his work in what category?

    a. Outstanding Costume Design of a Musical
    b. Outstanding Projection Design
    c. Outstanding Scenic Design of a Musical
    d. Outstanding Puppet Design

12. The 2005 Broadway stage adaptation of the irreverent comedy *Monty Python and the Holy Grail* had a book, music, and lyrics all written by which former member of Monty Python?

    a. John Cleese
    b. Eric Idle
    c. Terry Gilliam
    d. Michael Palin

13. *Mamma Mia!* is one of the rare movie musicals where the movie was adapted from the musical, but it has enjoyed popularity both on stage and screen. Which country did *Mamma Mia* become the longest daily running show in the history of its theatre in 2008?

a. Greece
b. South Korea
c. Russia
d. Mexico

14. True or False: The 2002 stage adaptation of *Thoroughly Modern Millie* featured television personality Meredith Vieira.

15. *Across the Universe*, a 2007 jukebox musical film written around the discography of popular band The Beatles, was directed by which female director who knows her way around a musical?

a. Susan Stroman
b. Julie Taymor
c. Kathryn Bigelow
d. Barbara Streisand

16. There are a few differences between the 2000 musical and the 1997 British film *The Full Monty*. The movie takes place in Sheffield, England while the musical takes place in what American city?

a. Boston, MA
b. Syracuse, NY
c. Buffalo, NY
d. Philadelphia, PA

17. The 2001 film *Moulin Rouge!* is the third film in the "Red Curtain Trilogy," the first three films directed by which Australian writer and filmmaker?

a. Peter Weir
b. George Miller

c. Warwick Thornton

d. Baz Luhrmann

18. True or False: Singer Mandy Moore choreographed the hit 2016 movie musical *La La Land*.

19. Her Broadway credits include *Rock of Ages*, *Kiss Me, Kate*, and *Chicago*. In 2006, she originated the role of Holly in the musical adaptation of *The Wedding Singer*. Who is this Broadway actress, who originated the role of Susan in the off-Broadway production of Jonathan Larson's *tick... tick...BOOM!*?

a. Laura Benanti

b. Alice Ripley

c. Emily Skinner

d. Amy Spanger

20. Frequent collaborators Jack O'Brien and Jerry Mitchell put their heads together as director and choreographer for the 2005 stage adaptation of *Dirty Rotten Scoundrels* which featured Norbert Leo Butz as Freddy Benson, Sherie Rene Scott as Christine Colgate, and what American actor known for his TV and film career?

a. Robert Lindsay

b. John Lithgow

c. Brian d'Arcy James

d. Boyd Gaines

ANSWERS

1. B - Ashley Brown

2. False! Mel Brooks was unsure if she would be able to play the role consistently due to her age, though she did reprise her performance for the show's first table reading.

3. C - *Catch Me If You Can*

4. D - Dolly Parton

5. A - Laura Bell Bundy

6. D - Heelys

7. A - Chester Gregory II

8. D - Elton John

9. False! The color-blind casting drew criticism from the American Anti-Arab Discrimination Committee who remarked that the show could have featured Middle Eastern actors who are underrepresented on Broadway.

10. A - John Waters

11. D - Outstanding Puppet Design

12. B - Eric Idle

13. C - Russia

14. True! During one performance on April 2, 2003, Meredith Vieira appeared in

15. three minor roles, which was filmed and broadcast for her popular daytime talk

16. show *The View*.

17. B - Julie Taymor

18. C - Buffalo, NY

19. D - Baz Luhrmann

20. False! Mandy Moore did choreograph *La La Land*, but the famous

21. choreographer who named her corporation "Nope Not Her," is vocal about being

22. confused with the better-known singer.

23. D - Amy Spanger

24. B - John Lithgow

DID YOU KNOW?

- Movie musicals were popularized during the 1930s in part due to the films of Busby Berkeley, whose kaleidoscopic shots of regimented lines of showgirls can be seen in films like *Footlight Parade* and *42nd Street*.

- Victor Fleming's *The Wizard of Oz* is one of the most beloved movie musicals of all time, and the film achieved landmark status due to its experimental new technology, like Technicolor.

- Movie musicals of the 1940s and 1950s owed part of their popularity to the movie's stars. It was important to have a big name to carry a movie musical, like Gene Kelly in *Singin' in the Rain* or Judy Garland in *Meet Me in St. Louis*.

- Many Rodgers and Hammerstein shows were made into movie musicals, like *Oklahoma!* in 1955, *The King and I*, which won five Academy Awards, in 1956, *Carousel* in 1956, and *South Pacific* in 1958.

- Rodgers and Hammerstein wrote their own movie musical as well, *State Fair*, which was a 1945 musical adaptation of the 1933 film. Their song "It Might As Well Be Spring" won the Academy Award for Best Original Song.

- Otto Preminger directed *Carmen Jones* in 1954 and *Porgy and Bess* in 1959, two movie musicals with Black casts that starred Dorothy Dandridge, who is often considered the first Black A-list film star.

- The 1960s marked the introduction of a few, very commercially successful movie musicals, like the 1961 film adaptation of *West Side Story* that became the highest-grossing film of 1961 and won ten Academy Awards, setting a record for the most wins for a musical.

- The 1964 film adaptation of *My Fair Lady* became the highest-grossing film of 1964 and won eight Academy Awards, and the 1965 film adaptation of *The Sound of Music* became the highest-grossing film of 1965, won five Academy Awards, and by November 1966 was the highest-grossing film of all time, a record that it held for five years.

- The abandonment of the Motion Picture Production Code, known as the Hays code, in 1968, led to changing attitudes towards film. Movie musicals that did well during this time period tended to be grittier or use rock-and-roll, like the 1973 film *Jesus Christ Superstar*, the 1978 film adaptation of *Grease*, and *All That Jazz*, a semi-autobiographical film directed by Bob Fosse.

- When *Chicago* won Best Picture at the Academy Awards in 2003, it became the first musical since *Oliver!* in 1968 to win the award.

CHAPTER 13:

NAME THAT SONG!

"I have a dream, a song to sing/ That helps me cope with anything /If you see the wonder of a fairy tale/ You can take the future, even if you fail." - Mamma Mia!

TRIVIA TIME!

1. "My sister and I had an act that couldn't flop / My sister and I were headed straight for the top / My sister and I earned a thou a week, at least / Oh sure! / But my sister is now, unfortunately, deceased."

    a. "I Will Never Leave You" from *Side Show*
    b. "Bosom Buddies" from *Mame*
    c. "I Can't Do It Alone" from *Chicago*
    d. "The Story of Lucy and Jessie" from *Follies*

2. "Nobody ever treated me kindly / Father left early, Mama was poor / I'd meet a man and I'd follow him blindly / He'd snap his fingers. Me, I'd say, sure."

    a. "Suddenly Seymour" from *Little Shop of Horrors*
    b. "As Long As He Needs Me" from *Oliver!*

c. "Some People" from *Gypsy*

d. "I'm Leaving You" from *The Life*

3. "Your sword could be a sermon / Or the power of the pen / Teach every child to raise his voice / And then my brothers, then / Will justice be demanded by ten million righteous men."

   a. "Red and Black" from *Les Misérables*

   b. "Run, Freedom, Run!" from *Urinetown*

   c. "And The Money Kept Rolling In (And Out)" from *Evita*

   d. "Make Them Hear You" from *Ragtime*

4. "A lady never leaves her escort / It isn't fair, it isn't nice / A lady doesn't wander all over the room / And blow on some other guy's dice."

   a. "Cold Feets" from *The Drowsy Chaperone*

   b. "Luck Be a Lady" from *Guys and Dolls*

   c. "Standing on the Corner" from *The Most Happy Fella*

   d. "I Can Cook Too" from *On the Town*

5. "When I get really lonely / And the distance calls its only silence / I think of you smiling / With pride in your eyes / A lover that sighs."

   a. "Sun and Moon" from *Miss Saigon*

   b. "If You Want Me" from *Once*

   c. "With You" from *Ghost*

   d. "Raining" from *Rocky*

6. "Nothing is so good it lasts eternally / Perfect situations must go wrong / But this has never yet prevented me / Wanting far too much for far too long."

a. "Stranger to the Rain" from *Children of Eden*
b. "Written in the Stars" from *Aida*
c. "The Winner Takes It All" from *Mamma Mia*
d. "I Know Him So Well" from *Chess*

7. "When I work in the mill weaving at the loom / I gaze absent-minded at the roof / And half the time the shuttle get tangled in the threads / And the warp would get mixed with the woof."

   a. "If I Loved You" from *Carousel*
   b. "Can't Help Lovin' Dat Man" from *Show Boat*
   c. "Lilacs" from *Preludes*
   d. "Wouldn't It Be Loverly?" from *My Fair Lady*

8. "You're the nimble tread of the feet of Fred Astaire / You're an O'Neill drama / You're Whistler's mama / You're camembert."

   a. "I Got Rhythm" from *Of Thee I Sing*
   b. "You're the Top" from *Anything Goes*
   c. "Too Darn Hot" from *Kiss Me, Kate*
   d. "Begin the Beguine" from *Jubilee*

9. "It's a very short road / From the pinch and the punch / To the paunch and the pouch and the pension / It's a very short road to the ten thousandth lunch / And the belch and the grouch and the sigh."

   a. "On the Steps of the Palace" from *Into the Woods*
   b. "(Not) Getting Married Today" from *Company*
   c. "I'm Still Here" from *Follies*
   d. "The Miller's Son" from *A Little Night Music*

10. "Every time I look at you, I don't understand / Why you let the things you did get so out of hand / You'd have managed better if you'd had it planned / Now why'd you choose such a backward time and such a strange land?"

    a. "Superstar" from *Jesus Christ Superstar*

    b. "Finale" from *Godspell*

    c. "Any Dream Will Do" from *Joseph and the Amazing Technicolor Dreamcoat*

    d. "In Whatever Time We Have" from *Children of Eden*

11. "If I'm wise / I will walk away / And gladly / But sadly / I'm not wise / It's hard to tuck away the mem'ries that you prize."

    a. "You Love Who You Love" from *Bonnie and Clyde*

    b. "In His Eyes" from *Jekyll & Hyde*

    c. "I'll Forget You" from *The Scarlet Pimpernel*

    d. "The Honor of Your Name" from *The Civil War*

12. "I believe I have inside of me / Everything that I need to live a bountiful life / And all the love alive in me / I'll stand as tall as the tallest tree / And I'm thankful for every day that I'm given / Both the easy and hard ones I'm livin'."

    a. "Back to Before" from *Ragtime*

    b. "I'm Here" from *The Color Purple*

    c. "I Know Where I've Been" from *Hairspray*

    d. "Listen" from *Dreamgirls*

13. "Harmony and understanding / Sympathy and trust abounding / No more falsehoods or derisions / Golden living dreams of visions / Mystic crystal revelation / And the mind's true liberation."

a. "Heaven on Their Minds" from *Jesus Christ Superstar*

b. "The Acid Queen" from *The Who's Tommy*

c. "Aquarius" from *Hair*

d. "Homecoming" from *American Idiot*

14. "You're here / That's all I need to know / And you will keep me safe / And you will keep me close / And rain will make the flowers grow."

a. "The Last Night of the World" from *Miss Saigon*

b. "Memory" from *Cats*

c. "A Little Fall of Rain" from *Les Misérables*

d. "Those You've Known" from *Spring Awakening*

15. "Come taste the wine / Come hear the band / Come blow a horn / Start celebrating / Right this way / Your table's waiting."

a. "Big Spender" from *Sweet Charity*

b. "Cabaret" from *Cabaret*

c. "Come to the Fun Home" from *Fun Home*

d. "Whatever Lola Wants" from *Damn Yankees*

16. "Gayer than laughter are you / Sweeter than music are you / Sunlight and moon beams / Heaven and earth / Are you to give me / And when your youth and joy / Invade my soul / And fill my heart / As now they do, then..."

a. "Younger than Springtime" from *South Pacific*

b. "Something Wonderful" from *The King and I*

c. "It Might As Well Be Spring" from *State Fair*

d. "Maria" from *West Side Story*

17. "Now's your inning. Stand the world on its ear! / Set it spinning! That'll be just the beginning! / Curtain up! Light the lights! / You've got nothing to hit but the heights!"

   a. "There's No Business Like Show Business" from *Annie Get Your Gun*
   b. "Don't Rain on My Parade" from *Funny Girl*
   c. "Show Off" from *The Drowsy Chaperone*
   d. "Everything's Coming Up Roses" from *Gypsy*

18. "An' the next thing ya know / Your son is playin' for money / In a pinch-back suit / And list'nin' to some big out-a-town jasper / Hearin' him tell about horse-race gamblin'."

   a. "The Oldest Established" from *Guys and Dolls*
   b. "Ya Got Trouble" from *The Music Man*
   c. "Rain Song" from *110 in the Shade*
   d. "I Won't Send Roses" from *Mack and Mabel*

19. "And how you're always turning back too late / From the grass or the stick / Or the dog or the light / How the kind of woman willing to wait's / Not the kind that you want to find waiting / To return you to the night / Dizzy from the height."

   a. "Finishing the Hat" from *Sunday in the Park with George*
   b. "Why" from *tick...tick...BOOM!*
   c. "Telephone Wire" from *Fun Home*
   d. "Dust and Ashes" from *Natasha, Pierre, and the Great Comet of 1812*

20. "We start with stars in our eyes / We start believing that we belong / But every sun doesn't rise / And no one tells

you where you went wrong / Step out, step out of the sun / If you keep getting burned."

    a. "Pretty Funny" from *Dogfight*

    b. "Waving Through a Window" from *Dear Evan Hansen*

    c. "The Meaning of Happiness" from *Daddy Long Legs*

    d. "Someone Gets Hurt" from *Mean Girls*

21. "Strangely quiet, but now the storm / Simply rests to strike again / Standing, waiting, I think of her / I think of her."

    a. "Lily's Eyes" from *The Secret Garden*

    b. "Fantine's Death" from *Les Misérables*

    c. "Color and Light" from *Sunday in the Park with George*

    d. "Marry Me a Little" from *Company*

22. "Oh, now I believe in lookin' / Like my time on earth is cookin' / Whether polka dotted, striped, or even checked / With some glamour guaranteeing / Every fiber of my being / Is displayed to quite remarkable effect."

    a. "Gorgeous" from *The Apple Tree*

    b. "Charming" from *Natasha, Pierre, and the Great Comet of 1812*

    c. "My Strongest Suit" from *Aida*

    d. "Dancing Through Life" from *Wicked*

23. "And when you least expect / Opportunity comes through the door / You suddenly connect / With the thing that you forgot / That you were looking for / And there you are / Right in the middle of what you love."

    a. "Hey #3/Perfect for You (Reprise)" from *Next to Normal*

b. "Everything I Know" from *In the Heights*

c. "Legally Blonde Remix" from *Legally Blonde*

d. "A Way Back to Then" from *[title of show]*

24. "Do they think that walls can hide you? / Even now I'm at your window / I am in the dark beside you / Buried sweetly in your yellow hair."

a. "Johanna" from *Sweeney Todd: The Demon Barber of Fleet Street*

b. "Later" from *A Little Night Music*

c. "Agony" from *Into the Woods*

d. "What Do I Need with Love" from *Thoroughly Modern Millie*

25. "I've hardly met a single soul, but I am not alone / I feel grown / This is wanting something, this praying for it / This is holding breath and keeping fingers crossed / This is counting blessings, this is wondering when I'll see that boy again."

a. "Gimme Gimme" from *Thoroughly Modern Millie*

b. "Waiting for Life to Begin" from *Once on This Island*

c. "The Beauty Is" from *The Light in the Piazza*

d. "Always Better" from *The Bridges of Madison County*

26. "Send me flowers / Mention is made / Make them roses / Attention is paid in full / See how quickly he sours / When he pushes I pull."

a. "Three Letters" from *She Loves Me*

b. "The Thrill of First Love" from *Falsettos*

c. "Wish I Were Here" from *Next to Normal*

d. "Loud" from *Matilda the Musical*

27. "That boy is staring and I feel a chill / I don't know why / That boy is staring and the world is still / Not tumbling by, there's no one talking / But I can hear a thousand voices / What's going on inside me? / That boy is staring, is it me he sees?"

    a. "Time Stops" from *Big Fish*
    b. "Come to a Party" from *Dogfight*
    c. "When He Sees Me" from *Waitress*
    d. "Fight For Me" from *Heathers*

28. "Many a like lad may kiss and fly / A kiss gone by is bygone / Never have I asked an August sky / 'Where has last July gone?' / Never have I wandered through the rye / Wondering where has some guy gone."

    a. "I'm Gonna Wash That Man Right Outa My Hair" from *South Pacific*
    b. "Forget About the Boy" from *Thoroughly Modern Millie*
    c. "I Hate Men" from *Kiss Me, Kate*
    d. "Many a New Day" from *Oklahoma!*

29. "Some people analyze every detail / Some people stall when they can't see the trail / Some people freeze out of fear that they'll fail / But I keep rolling on / Some people can't find success with their art / Some people never feel love in their heart / Some people can't tell the two things apart / But I keep rolling on."

    a. "Moving Too Fast" from *The Last 5 Years*
    b. "Some People" from *Gypsy*
    c. "Why" from *tick...tick...BOOM!*
    d. "Subway" from *Preludes*

30. "Awful sweet to be a little butterfly / Just swinging over things and nothing deep inside / Nothing going, going wild in you, you know / You're slowing by the riverside, a-floating high and blue."

    a. "Don't Do Sadness/Blue Wind" from *Spring Awakening*
    b. "All Grown Up" from *Bare*
    c. "Any Way the Wind Blows" from *Hadestown*
    d. "If You Knew My Story" from *Bright Star*

31. "The men in this town / Live and die and are forgotten / And it doesn't seem to scare 'em / I can't wait to get away / Away from the drought / And the homeless and the hungry / Where they talk / About foreclosures / Every hot and dusty day."

    a. "Someday" from *The Civil War*
    b. "The World Will Remember Me" from *Bonnie and Clyde*
    c. "A Man's Gotta Do" from *Bright Star*
    d. "Do You Wanna Go to Heaven" from *Big River*

32. "I'm tingling, such delicious tingles / I'm trembling, what the hell does that mean? / I'm freezing, that's because it's cold out / And still I'm incandescent / And like some adolescent / I'd like to scrawl on every wall I see."

    a. "That'll Show Him" from *A Funny Thing Happened on the Way to the Forum*
    b. "Ladies In Their Sensitivities" from *Sweeney Todd: The Demon Barber of Fleet Street*
    c. "She Loves Me" from *She Loves Me*
    d. "As If We Never Said Goodbye" from *Sunset Boulevard*

33. "What else is there to do / But plant the seed / And pull the weed / And chop the cane / And bear the child / And bear the load / And bear the pain / And as the rich go racing to their own refrain..."

    a. "We Dance" from *Once On This Island*
    b. "Extraordinary" from *Pippin*
    c. "Sal Tlay Ka Siti" from *The Book of Mormon*
    d. "A Rumor in St. Petersburg" from *Anastasia*

34. "Day after day / Wishing all our cares away / Trying to fight the things we feel / But some hurts never heal / Some ghosts are never gone / But we go on / We still go on / And you find some way to survive / And you find out you don't have to be happy at all / To be happy you're alive."

    a. "Another Winter in a Summer Town" from *Grey Gardens*
    b. "Seventeen (Reprise)" from *Heathers*
    c. "Homecoming" from *American Idiot*
    d. "Light" from *Next to Normal*

35. "Why do we stay with lovers / Who we know down deep / Just aren't right / Why would we rather / Put ourselves through Hell / Than sleep alone at night?"

    a. "Fly, Fly Away" from *Catch Me If You Can*
    b. "Louder than Words" from *tick...tick...BOOM!*
    c. "Always Starting Over" from *If/Then*
    d. "Finale B" from *RENT*

ANSWERS

1. C - "I Can't Do It Alone" from *Chicago*

2. A - "Suddenly Seymour" from *Little Shop of Horrors*

3. D - "Make Them Hear You" from *Ragtime*

4. B - "Luck Be a Lady" from *Guys and Dolls*

5. B - "If You Want Me" from *Once*

6. D - "I Know Him So Well" from *Chess*

7. A - "If I Loved You" from *Carousel*

8. B - "You're the Top" from *Anything Goes*

9. D - "The Miller's Son" from *A Little Night Music*

10. A - "Superstar" from *Jesus Christ Superstar*

11. B - "In His Eyes" from *Jekyll & Hyde*

12. B - "I'm Here" from *The Color Purple*

13. C - "Aquarius" from *Hair*

14. C - "A Little Fall of Rain" from *Les Misérables*

15. B - "Cabaret" from *Cabaret*

16. A - "Younger than Springtime" from *South Pacific*

17. D - "Everything's Coming Up Roses" from *Gypsy*

18. B - "Ya Got Trouble" from *The Music Man*

19. A - "Finishing the Hat" from *Sunday in the Park with George*

20. B - "Waving Through a Window" from *Dear Evan Hansen*

21. A - "Lily's Eyes" from *The Secret Garden*

22. C - "My Strongest Suit" from *Aida*

23. D - "A Way Back to Then" from *[title of show]*

24. A - "Johanna" from *Sweeney Todd: The Demon Barber of Fleet Street*

25. C - "The Beauty Is" from *The Light in the Piazza*

26. B - "The Thrill of First Love" from *Falsettos*

27. A - "Time Stops" from *Big Fish*

28. D - "Many a New Day" from *Oklahoma!*

29. A - "Moving Too Fast" from *The Last 5 Years*

30. A - "Don't Do Sadness/Blue Wind" from *Spring Awakening*

31. B - "This World Will Remember Me" from *Bonnie and Clyde*

32. B - "She Loves Me" from *She Loves Me*

33. A - "We Dance" from *Once On This Island*

34. D - "Light" from *Next to Normal*

35. B - "Louder Than Words" from *tick...tick...BOOM!*

Made in the USA
Las Vegas, NV
11 November 2021

34111191R00085